I Wish I'd Said That!

Dr Maurice A. Silver was born in Glasgow, Scotland. He has been an engineer and a salesman and has held various management posts. It is difficult to get him to accept anything at face value; he insists on thinking about it and if he believes it could be improved, he tries to revise it. He shares his time between Glasgow and southern Spain and has one son.

I Wish I'd Said That!

An Entertaining Collection of
Wise Thoughts and Witty Sayings

Maurice A. Silver

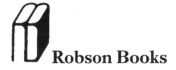

Robson Books

This book is dedicated to the memory of my parents, Bernard and Celia Silver.

First published in Great Britain in 1999 by Robson Books,
10 Blenheim Court, Brewery Road, London N7 9NT

A member of the Chrysalis Group plc

British Library Cataloguing in Publication Data
A catalogue record for this title is available from the British Library

ISBN 1 86105 285 5

Typeset in Ehrhardt by SX Composing DTP, Rayleigh, Essex
Printed and bound in Great Britain by Creative Print & Design
(Wales) Ltd.

CONTENTS

ACKNOWLEDGEMENTS

I would like to thank John Ashley and David Watt for their considerable help and patience, and their technical expertise in helping to put this book together.

Introduction

This is not just another book of quotations.

My book contains a very wide selection of thoughts and sayings that have been gathered over a period of more than fifty years. Some of these quotes will be familiar to the reader, but a large number have more obscure origins. Wherever possible, the source of the item has been acknowledged but there are many entries where this is unknown. In all unsourced cases, due apologies are sincerely offered to the originator.

The quotes in this book are slotted into three hundred and fifty categories thus allowing the reader to quickly and easily find something relevant to a particular situation. The material ranges from simple one-line, thought-provoking utterances to fairly serious one-paragraph philosophies. Some are humorous, some are serious and many are included because they should make you sit back and think.

It would be both foolish and impossible to attempt to compile a book which would be all things to all people. That which stirs one person may leave another wholly unmoved. However there is nothing to stop you adapting or modifying any of the entries to suit your own requirements. One of them may be just right for your particular circumstances.

A brilliant Nobel Prize winner, Richard Feynman, used to work on the basis that when giving a lecture there was no way he could capture the attention of his audience all of the time. Feynman took the attitude that if he could include a wide enough range of 'hooks' in his lecture then he stood a good chance of making his lecture interesting for most of his audience, most of the time. I have used a similar approach. The large number of categories allows the reader to look for something of relevance – a key expression, a 'hook', a challenge, an opener with a punch – to use at a meeting, an interview, or in discussion.

The entries are not cross-indexed because that would pad out the book unnecessarily. The main criterion for inclusion in a category is the primary topic of the entry. However, please be willing to search around in different categories for the quote you are looking for.

I would ask you not to prejudge this collection. It would be better if you were to pick specific categories of interest, or groups of categories, and read them, rather than merely flicking through the pages. If you find just one item that brings a smile to your face, assists your speech/text or makes you muse over what you have read, then I consider that I have achieved my aim.

I do hope that you find pleasure and assistance from my efforts.

Maurice A. Silver

ABILITY

Ability is the power of applying knowledge to practical purposes.

Men of great abilities are generally of a large and vigorous animal nature.

It is safe to assume that the vast majority of able people will achieve at least some measure of success and recognition.

ACCEPTANCE

What's done is done, and what's won is won; and what is lost is gone for ever.

When you're in a hole, stop digging.
Michael Rowley

Don't count on anybody else coming along to relieve your stress. Put yourself in charge of managing the situation.
Price Pritchett, Ron Pound

Some things we just need to accept. Sometimes the real wisdom lies in resigning ourselves to a situation, even if we don't like it.
Price Pritchett, Ron Pound

Trying to control matters that we personally can't control is a pure waste of time. It's a bad investment of our psychological energy.

Price Pritchett, Ron Pound

ACHIEVEMENT

Can you walk on water? You have done no better than a straw. Can you fly in the air? You have done no better than a bluebottle. Conquer your heart; then you may become somebody.

Ansari of Herat

If the young man knew how and the old man was able, there would be nothing which wouldn't be done.

People don't remember the calibre of your opposition; they remember only the grade you achieved.

To be born a gentleman is an accident, but to die a gentleman is an achievement.

If you can imagine it, you can achieve it. If you can dream it, you can become it.

William Ward

Pushing events to happen before their time is less important than their ultimate achievement.

Wess Roberts

It is better to have lived one day as a tiger than a thousand years as a sheep.

Tibetan saying

'Well done' is better than 'Well said'.

Benjamin Franklin

Talk is cheap – people are judged by deeds.

ACRONYMS

B.F.I. Brute force and ignorance.

B.M.C. Blue moon circumstances.

K.I.S.S. Keep it short, stupid.

They were going to call it the Sam Houston Institute of Technology but decided that it wouldn't look good on the T-shirts, so its name was changed to the Dallas Technical College.

L.B.W. file Let the buggers wait.

David Cooper

N.I.M.B.Y. Not in my back yard!

W.Y.S.I.W.Y.G. What you see is what you get.

Y.C.D.B.S.O.Y.A. You can't do business sitting on your ass.

Motorola Inc.

ACTIVITY

Better to wear out than rust out.

Basic research is what I am doing when I don't know what I'm doing.

Wernher von Braun

A really busy person never knows how much he weighs.

E.W. Howe

It's no good just thinking about a thing. You have to do it too.

It isn't doing the job that takes the time; it's the starting and the finishing of it.

If you try, you might. If you don't, you won't.

W. Pickles

In any given group, the most will do the least and the least the most.

Merle P. Martin

Just do a thing and don't talk about it. This is the great secret of success in all enterprises.

Normally, planning is essential, otherwise you get unconnected random activity. Planning involves much discussion and talking, but results come only from activity. No amount of talking ever built anything. Only action will produce results. By all means talk about it but motivate yourself to do something. Don't just talk about it – do it!
   And if not you, then who?
   And if not now, then when?

When I see others sweating in a health club I wonder if they're doing it because they don't have anywhere else to sweat.

Kim Woo-Choong

Those who threaten never do; those who do don't waste time threatening.

Tim Sebastian

Never mistake motion for action.

Ernest Hemingway

ADVANCEMENT

Everything you take for granted today was once revolutionary.

An Assistant Professor is a PhD who has learned to make a single point into a lecture, an Associate Professor is someone who has learned to make a point into a course, a Professor has learned to make a point into a whole career, a Dean has forgotten the point and a President thinks there never was a point.

Prof. John Crispo

The most profitable development of all is self-development.

Many are called, few are chosen; fewer still get to do the choosing.

Bryan K. Silver

A better quality of society is likely to be the follow-on of a prosperous society. A business doesn't open a social club when it is first set up. The social and sports club will be established only after the business has prospered. Similarly, an education system must first provide courses that will produce graduates who will make the nation stronger. Social science is a qualification which must follow the productive degrees. The nation will not suffer too much if there is a shortage of people qualified in basket weaving, clog dancing, flower arranging and napkin folding.

5

ADVERTISING

Advertising costs money, but being forgotten costs more.

Advertising is the most fun of anything you can do with your clothes on.

Mary Wells

Advertising is legalised lying.

H.G. Wells

ADVICE

The smartest person we know is the one who asks our advice.

Wise men don't need advice; fools won't take it.

Benjamin Franklin

Advice is like the snow – the more softly it falls, the better it takes hold.

We give advice, but we cannot give the wisdom to profit from it.

La Rochefoucauld

He who hesitates is lost. Oh really? And should we look before we leap? Which advice should we follow?

The first time you give bad advice it's excusable, the second time it's suspicious, but the third time it's enemy action.

Advice is seldom welcome, and those who need it the most always like it the least.

Earl of Chesterfield

Advice from a father to his son: 'Buy land, son. God has stopped making land but He is still making people.'

AGE

'I plan to live for 200 years.'
    'Good. I'll be one of your pall bearers.'

Angelo Fusco

Forty is the old age of youth, fifty is the youth of old age.

I seem to be growing old alone. My wife hasn't had a birthday for six years.

M. White

You're getting old when the girl you smile at thinks you're one of her father's friends.

A. Murray

Middle-age is when the narrow waist and broad mind begin to change places.

No man is really old until his mother stops worrying about him.

W. Ryan

Every man desires to live long; but no man would be old.

Being a miner, as soon as you're too old and tired and sick and stupid to do your job properly you have to go, whereas the very opposite applies with the judges.

Beyond the Fringe

Many a man that can't direct you to a corner drugstore will get a respectful hearing when age has further impaired his mind.

Finley Peter Dunne

Observations of an older railway man: 'At our age, we don't call stations "terminals" and we don't talk about expiry dates.'

Norman King

I don't think we get wiser with age. Wisdom is something inherent. But we get sly. I would say I am more cautious now than when I was younger, but otherwise I have no advantage over youth. Old age is not nice.

Enoch Powell

I am too old for change. I am too old to pursue good health and new relationships. The past breathes for me. It is my life. Someday you will see what it is like to look back. You will find your personal history drawing you back into familiar rooms where events occurred that set in motion your eventual estrangement from life. You will find the hard furniture of heartbreak more comfortable and the people who failed you, friendlier with time. You will find yourself running back into the arms of the pain you once ran away from. It is easier.

Patricia D. Cornwell

Old age is always fifteen years older than I am.

Bernard M. Baruch

How old would you be if you didn't know how old 'old' was?

I have everything I had twenty years ago, only it's all a little bit lower.

Gypsy Rose Lee

Age is all in your mind. The trick is to keep it from creeping down into your body.

AMBITION

Who at Oxford or Cambridge wants to start their own business, he asks. Yet at MIT, being your own boss is the ambition of almost everyone. And I am not talking about the UK, the whole of Europe is the same. The best and the brightest don't want to go into business. They don't want to roll up their sleeves and get on with it.

Birch

If you aspire to the highest place, it is no disgrace to stop at the second, or even the third.

Cicero

Every ambitious project requires a lot of resolution.

The trouble with my people is their poverty of desire.

Ernest Bevin

When I grow up, I want to be a beneficiary.

MAS

Everyone's got their own form of ambition.

The sorry desire for approbation, no matter what.

Campbell Armstrong

Don't sacrifice your life on the altar of career. The distance between success and failure can only be measured by one's desire.

I don't want to achieve immortality through my work; I want to achieve immortality through not dying.

Woody Allen

ANGER

Must the hunger become anger and the anger fury before anything will be done?

John Steinbeck

Anger and haste hinder good counsel.

Bad temper is its own scourge; it hurts a man more than his victim.

To be positive: to be mistaken at the top of one's voice.

N.M. Butler

There is always a reason for anger but rarely a good one.

It's the people who are in the wrong who get angry.

Napoleon

Never reply to a letter when in an angry mood.

When angry, count four; when very angry, swear.

Mark Twain

You know his wrath. It falls on the innocent as well as the guilty.

Clive Cussler

If someone does something that is not working you need to help the situation. If you respond with anger you can make it worse.

Robert Riley

Don't get angry, get even.

He that is slow to anger has great understanding.

Anger breeds false courage.

ANIMALS

Perhaps it's only coincidence, but man's best friend can't talk.

J. Cannon

Midges and jellyfish are good for bugger-all.

Fishing boat captain

There are two things for which animals are to envied: they know nothing of future evils nor of what people say about them.

Voltaire

ANSWERS

Don't give me an answer to a different question; give me an answer to the question I asked.

I think it's much more interesting to live not knowing, than to have answers which might be wrong.

Richard Feynman

The answer is a definite maybe.

APPLICATION

Those who say it cannot be done are usually interrupted by others doing it.

Elbert Hubbard

There is no substitute for thorough-going, ardent and sincere earnestness.

The proverb 'If at first you don't succeed, try, try, try again' should be altered to 'If at first you don't succeed, try another method.'

Look at a day when you are supremely satisfied at the end. It's not a day when you lounge around doing nothing; it's a day when you've had everything to do, and you've done it.

Margaret Thatcher

Some people dream of success while others wake up and work hard at it.

Don't wait for your ship to come in; swim out to it.

ARGUMENTS

You can't solve a quarrel by making a row about it.

A good argument has no need of a loud voice.

A quarrel wouldn't last long if the fault was all on one side.

Saying it louder doesn't make you any more right.

Bryan K. Silver

Use soft words but loud arguments.

Argument proceeds through seven stages – retort courteous, quip modest, reply churlish, reproof valiant, countercheck quarrelsome, lie circumstantial and lie direct – on its way to becoming deadly.

William Shakespeare

I'm not arguing, but you were wrong.

Sheila Biggs

You can't change people's minds by arguing with them.

In disagreements with loved ones, deal with the current situation. Don't bring up the past.

ARROGANCE

For a manager to espouse a job-specific programme of skills enhancement to apply, for example, to a machine operator or a draftsman, and decline to acknowledge his or her own needs as a manager, is arrogance indeed.

Ego is when a man, sitting in a crowded bus, flirts with a woman who is standing.

C. Melton

I thought I was wrong, but I was mistaken.

It is only a suggestion, but let's not forget who is making it.

Everyone's entitled to my opinion.

Without the remotest possibility of doubt.

Don't try to reason or argue about the decision. It is Company policy so just accept it.

Jos Graham-Smith

ART

Ancient marbles enrich a man for all his life; they open our eyes but take words away, with the result that our soul is wise, and nice and silent, as are they.

Ivo Andric

There are two ways of disliking art. One is to dislike it. The other is to like it rationally.

Oscar Wilde

Art does not reproduce the visible, but makes visible.

Paul Klee

ASSISTANCE

Never ask from one who has, but rather from one who loves you well.

People must help one another; it is Nature's law.

La Fontaine

It's a good thing to give a poor man a fish to eat, but it is better to teach him how to fish.

I don't think you should assume that an injection of money solves everyone's problems.

Kenneth Clarke

ATTITUDES TO LIFE

The public school canon: never complain, never explain.

If you're going to walk in front, lead. If you're going to walk behind, follow. But if you're just going to stand there, get the hell out of the way.

The crab more than any of God's creatures has formulated the perfect philosophy of life. Whenever he is confronted by a great moral crisis in life, he first makes up his mind what is right, and then goes sideways as fast as he can.

Oliver Herford

March towards the sound of gunfire.

Keep facing the sun, and the shadows will fall behind you.

A pessimist says 'There's a cloud in front of the sun.' An optimist says 'Behind the cloud is the sun.'

Don't jump on a man unless he's down.

Finley Peter Dunne

Look British, think Yiddish.

Harvard Business School

Tomorrow's the first day of the rest of my life – and that's true for you too. Stop looking over your shoulder and start looking forward.

Bob Seelert

Do it today – tomorrow it might be illegal.

Don't take yourself too seriously.

Robert Louis Stevenson

The generous man likes to speak well of other people. The petty man prefers to run them down.

Confucius

Contemporary tradition; that's the way we did it last time.

Attitude is everything.

Attitude is a little thing that makes a big difference.

ATTRACTIVENESS

Rabbit food may be good for executives. Middle-aged rabbits don't have a paunch, have their own teeth and haven't lost their romantic appeal.

Dr A. Poter

Ever notice that a girl with bad legs never sees a mouse?

E. Miller

I believe a little incompatibility is the spice of life, particularly if he has income and she is pattable.

Ogden Nash

There is nothing so attractive to a man as a woman obviously available.

Michael Sinclair

Men are propelled by desire for attractive women.

Colin Forbes

AWARENESS

The novelist is terribly exposed to life. He can no more cease to receive impressions than a fish in mid-ocean can cease to let the water run through his gills.

Virginia Woolf

Men occasionally stumble over the truth, but most of them pick themselves up and hurry off as if nothing had happened.

Winston S. Churchill

Arguing with a warranty clerk (or a tour operator, or an insurance assessor, or whatever) is like wrestling with a pig in the mud. After a while, you realise that the pig enjoys it.

Look both ways, even in a one-way street.

Common sense is the least common of the senses.

You don't have to eat the whole cow to know the meat is bad.

Dr Johnson

We spend so much of our lives looking upwards, motivated by a mixture of ambition and envy. Occasionally, you should look down; there are far more people below you than there are above you.

Philip Zolkwer

BACHELORS

A bachelor is a man who never Mrs anybody.

T. Stone

The best training for bachelorhood is marriage.

A bachelor is a man who only has to make one breakfast before going to work.

A. Herbert

BARGAINS

There is no such thing in life as a bargain.

There is no such thing as a free lunch.

A bargain is only a bargain if it is something you wanted, and were going to buy anyway.

BEAUTY

She's rather like Venus de Milo – beautiful, but not all there.

I'm tired of all this nonsense about beauty being only skin-deep. That's deep enough. What do you want – an adorable pancreas?

Jean Kerr

Remember always that the least plain sister is the family beauty.

George Bernard Shaw

BED

The hardest people to convince they are at retiring age are children at bedtime.

There are substitutes for almost everything except work and sleep.

We can heat the body, we can cool it; we can give it tension or relaxation; and surely it is possible to bring it into a state in which rising from bed will not be a pain.

James Boswell

There ought to be a better way to start the day than by getting up in the morning.

R. Wilson

Laugh and the world laughs with you; snore, and you sleep alone.

In bed we laugh, in bed we cry
And born in bed, in bed we die.

BEHAVIOUR

A person can be said to dress/behave/act well only if that is his standard, consistent manner. The infrequent exhibition of such manner, such as wearing a suit on Sunday only, in no way qualifies the person as being well dressed.

MAS

You will find rest from vain fancies if you do every act in life as though it were your last.

Aurelius

The drawback in setting a good example for your own children is that it takes all the fun out of your own middle-age.

Always do right. It will gratify some people and astonish the rest.

If you cannot be chaste, be careful.

Doing what you want isn't always doing what you ought to.

If a man does not keep pace with his companions, perhaps it is because he hears a different drummer. Let him step to the music which he hears, however measured or far away.

H.D. Thoreau

Do as I say, not as I do.

We think according to Nature,
We speak according to rules,
But we act according to custom.

Bacon

It is impossible, in our conditions of society, not to be sometimes a snob.

Thackeray

Never regret, never explain, and never apologise.

Benjamin Jowett

Actions are the ultimate expression of a man. Once a thing is done you can't just scrub it out. It's there, like a rope round your neck.

Hammond Innes

Men and nations behave wisely once they have exhausted all the other alternatives.

Abba Eban

BELIEF

How sweet it is to hear one's own convictions from a stranger's mouth.

Goethe

'I don't believe you.'
'I have no control over what you believe or don't believe.'

Some people will believe anything if it is whispered to them.

The moment someone disagrees or objects to what you are saying, that will be the moment you will suddenly recognise the strength of your belief.

Marjorie Phillips

BITTERNESS

If sons of bitches could fly, you wouldn't see the sun.

She is evenly balanced – she has a chip on both shoulders.

Gill Paul

Bitterness doesn't do anyone any good, it just destroys the soul.

William Ronald Miller

BLAME

Only the old may prophesy safely. They will not be around to take the blame if they are wrong!

The easiest hunt is the hunt to find a scapegoat.

Dwight Eisenhower

The dominant desire of the institution concerned is to avoid blame, rather than exercise responsibility.

The practice of blaming objects is nothing more than a deceptive, quack cure, which prevents us from searching for a real solution to society's ills.

Philip Cook

There is no point blaming the world because you can't change it.

Concentrate on fixing the problem, not on apportioning the blame.

Japanese proverb

Finding and placing blame ranks above football and sex as our favourite pastime.

Robert Andrews

You may believe you'll be a better victim if you find somebody else to blame, someone you can accuse of causing your problems; by doing that, you shift the accountability for your behaviour and attitude away from yourself.

Price Pritchett, Ron Pound

BOATS

Every man wants a boat four feet longer than the one he's got.

Arthur Yaffy

Oh God, thy sea is so great and my boat is so small.

Boating is not a matter of life or death; it's more important than that.

If you counted the cost of running a boat you'd shoot yourself. It's a money box with two holes in the bottom.

Sir Freddie Laker

BOOKS

A house without books is like a room without windows.

To destroy the Western tradition of independent thought it is not necessary to burn the books. All we have to do is to leave them unread for a couple of generations.

R.M. Hutchins

A book is a success when people who haven't read it pretend they have.

J. McCarthy

A classic is something that everyone wants to have read and nobody wants to read.

Mark Twain

A library is the most precious of all possessions.

The man who does not read good books has no advantage over the man who cannot read them.

Mark Twain

BOREDOM

The secret of being a bore is to tell everything.

Voltaire

If, at the end of two or three minutes you haven't struck oil, give up boring.

J.R. Lowell

The chief product of a highly automated society is a widespread and deepening sense of boredom. People should be forbidden by law to work more than three days a week at computers or other kinds of automated equipment.

C. Northcote Parkinson

Dogs make you walk, politics makes you think. Only boredom makes you old.

Baroness Barbara Castle

BREEDING

A gentleman is a man who will never knowingly cause grief or pain to another.

Good manners are the happy way of doing things.

One of the marks of a gentleman is his refusal to make an issue out of every difference of opinion.

A.H. Glasgow

The first to fall silent in a quarrel comes from the better family.

The test of good manners: to bear patiently with bad ones.

Merit and good breeding will make their way everywhere.

Good manners consist of small sacrifices.

Ralph Waldo Emerson

Manners are the mark of a better man.

'Why are you so goddamn polite?'
'For the same reason you are not; it's the way I was brought up.'

He is a good man who can receive a gift well.

Bad manners are the enemy of freedom.

W.F. Deedes

Good manners cost nothing, but giving them up represents a sad decline in the quality of life. There is much to be learned by remembering about the man who stood and offered his seat to a woman on a train. She fainted. When she recovered she thanked him. He fainted.

BRIBERY

It is better to be bribed than to bribe.

If you don't grease, you can't slide.

Ivor Higgins

BUSINESS

Myriad small businesses, which together, let us never forget, employ 35 per cent of the labour force.

The craft of the merchant is this: bringing a thing from where it abounds to where it is costly.

Ralph Waldo Emerson

Business is like a wheelbarrow.
Nothing ever happens until you start pushing.

Your competitor gives you a free lesson in what you must, but also in what you must not, do.

It is easier to start a business than to keep it going.

Never hire who you can't fire.

Eric Reid

My father told me that all businessmen were sons of bitches, but I never believed him until now.

John F. Kennedy

Men are mortal, but giant corporations are sacred to eternity.

Morris West

CARS

Taxi: Vehicle that always seems to dissolve in the rain.

D. Bennett

A Rolls-Royce is a statement. A Bentley is an understatement.

In an expanding universe, why can't I find a parking space?

As wide open as the doors of a car on the showroom floor.

CHANCE

A chance is a currency which will have devalued tomorrow.

One is nothing; two may be a coincidence; three is a trend.

If you will not when you may, you may not when you will.

Lily Hill

A stumbling block is a stepping-stone that you tripped over.

CHANGE

Concerning any new thing, never consult the man whose life it is about to change.

R. Loewy

Then there are the learned barriers. Psychologists refer to this problem as 'functional fixedness'. A common manifestation is the attitude that there is only one way to do things – as a result of social conventions, possibilities, taboos. The way you know individuals who suffer with this problem is when you try to introduce something new, they will automatically say 'We can't do it that way!' Moreover, they will be unable to give you a reason why. Functional fixedness is tantamount to wearing intellectual and emotional blinkers.

Dr P.W. Buffington

Progress is impossible without change, and those who cannot change their minds cannot change anything.

George Bernard Shaw

Nothing so needs reforming as other people's habits.

Mark Twain

If change is planned it can happen naturally and be in everybody's interests. If it happens in a hurry, there are usually casualties.

If you truly want to understand something, try to change it.

THE GIANT JELLY SYNDROME
It is put forward that Glasgow University (or any large institution or business) can be likened to a giant jelly. The forces for change can attack the jelly with great effort and enthusiasm and

can surely make it move and wobble, and indeed appear to be changing; but after they have finished, it will settle right back, exactly, into its previous form.

Ray C. Welland

New doesn't necessarily mean better.

This is a changing world, and we must be prepared to change with it.

Paul Harris

Change is sometimes threatening.

Remember that change, halfway through, always looks like failure.

David Watt

CHARACTER

Character is what you are in the dark.

D.L. Moody

Character is the diamond that scratches every other stone.

The measure of a man's real character is what he would do if he knew he would never be found out.

In each human heart are a tiger, a pig, and a nightingale. Diversity of character is due to their unequal activity.

Ambrose Bierce

You should pick people for character. Intelligence you can always hire.

Henry Kissinger

You can mould a mannerism, but you must chisel a character.

A person's character is like a fence – it cannot be strengthened by whitewash.

A butler is a solemn procession made up of one man only.

Once an Admiral, always a son of a bitch.

CHARITY

I know that a man who shows me his wealth is like the beggar who shows me his poverty; they are both looking for alms from me, the rich man for the alms of my envy and the poor man for the alms of my guilt.

Ben Hecht

If you are not poor enough to take charity then you are rich enough to give it.

If you have money over and have no charity, you can well call yourself poor.

Charity brings bitterness and no respect on either side.

Take time to give. It is too short a day to be selfish.

Do what you can for those less fortunate than yourself.

Robert Louis Stevenson

When it comes to giving, some stop at nothing.

CHEATING

The first and worst of all frauds is to cheat one's self.

People who cheat in life may not necessarily cheat in golf, but people who cheat in golf always cheat in life.

Rabbi Marc Gellman

Copy from one, it's plagiarism; copy from two, it's research.

Wilson Mizner

CHILDREN

My children are at the perfect age – too old to cry at night and too young to borrow my car.

W. Slezak

I am very fond of children; especially girl children of about 16 or 17 years old.

W.C. Fields

Children grow by leaps and bounds, especially in the apartment overhead.

Many a sweater is worn by a child when his mother feels cold.

A child's greatest period of growth is the month after you have bought new school clothes.

If mother says 'No', ask grandma.

If you don't want your children to hear what you're saying, pretend you're talking to them.

CHOICE

Don't walk in front of me, I may not follow.
Don't walk behind me, I may not lead.
Walk beside me and just be my friend.

Camus

You can't have everything, so you must decide what you want most.

The hardest thing in life to learn is which bridge to cross and which to burn.

David Russell

CIVILIZATION

Judge a society by the way it treats its gypsies.

Alcoholism and race consciousness are two conspicuous sources of danger to Western civilization. A mixture of atheism, materialism, socialism and alcoholism have been the cause of the decline and decay of 19 out of 20 civilizations.

A. Toynbee

Civilization is a movement and not a condition; a voyage, and not a harbour.

A. Toynbee

The degree of civilization in a society can be judged by entering its prisons.

F. Dostoyevski

The regression of civilization could, perhaps, be measured by the increasing number of locks and keys and security devices with which we are now involved.

MAS

It is by behaviour rather than by material possessions that the quality of a civilization can best be judged.

It's very few steps from the village to the jungle.

Morris West

CLIMATE

The best thing about spring is that it comes when it is most needed.

Rain – what taxi drivers pray for and pedestrians pay for.

Springtime is the land awakening. The March winds are the morning yawn.

Lewis Grizzard

COERCION

To force opinion is like pushing the magnetised needle round until it points to where we wish the North Star stood.

D.C. Fisher

You have not converted a man because you have silenced him.

John Viscount Morley

Men may be convinced, but they cannot be pleased, against their will.

You can compel people to obey or to submit, but you cannot compel them to agree.

Winston S. Churchill

COMMITMENT

I will start by saying why I said that I would be pleased to come along and talk about this subject. It is quite simple: I believe in it passionately.

If you want to be a lumberjack, you must learn to carry your end of the log.

Value and productivity are generally associated with commitment . . . is the commitment there?

A fanatic is usually a waverer who has at last taken a decision.

There are no half-measures; we should go metric every inch of the way.

Nothing in this world is impossible to a willing heart.

Never doubt that a small group of thoughtful, committed people can change the world. Indeed, it is the only thing that ever has.

Remember that great love and great achievements involve great risk.

COMMITTEES

Every nation has the government it deserves . . . and every club has the committee it deserves.

Joseph De Maistre

A committee takes root and grows, it flowers, wilts and dies, scattering the seed from which other committees will bloom.

C. Northcote Parkinson

Consider the phenomenon that has often been observed but never yet investigated. It might be termed the Law of Triviality. Briefly stated, it means that the time spent on any item on the agenda will be in inverse proportion to the sum involved.

C. Northcote Parkinson

Committees: God's gift to procrastination, sloth and delay. Men of little flair compensate for their failure of imagination by banding together in groups called committees.

Campbell Armstrong

A committee keeps minutes and wastes hours.

Don't worry too much about trying to get your views accepted at a committee meeting. Just fake the minutes later on.

A camel is a horse designed by a committee.

Nothing is ever accomplished by a committee unless it is composed of three people, one of whom happens to be ill and another absent.

H. Van Loon

COMMUNICATION

Leadership goes with communication. They are indispensably linked if you use them properly.

'Dialogue' does not mean simply having a conversation with others. It means expressing one's own thoughts in a language that others can understand, and listening to what they have to say in return. Dialogue does not only mean exchange of ideas and communion of thought; it also means collaboration in deeds, exchange of help – it means service.

There are only two things a child will share willingly – communicable diseases and his mother's age.

Dr B. Spock

What we have here is a failure to communicate.

Please be a little more explicit.
We are on the same side, you know.

One of the quickest ways to meet new people is to pick up the wrong ball on a golf course.

We're not on the same wavelength; in fact we're not even beamed on the same satellite.

The message of the sunset is sadness; the message of the dawn is hope.

Winston S. Churchill

COMPROMISE

Be warned against superficial solutions and the easy compromises.

Find the bridge between the past and the future; between expectation and reality; between potential and fulfilment. And totally reject short-term compromises. As the Chinese proverb says: 'It is sometimes unwise, when crossing a chasm, to attempt it in two stages.'

I am aware of the beatification accorded to compromise. Seductive as it is to be on the side of the angels, I see very little role for compromise in planning. You cannot have half a Channel Tunnel. Perhaps we shall find out to our cost in the next five years that you cannot half devolve.

Compromise is the art of dividing a cake so that everyone thinks he has got the biggest slice.

COMPUTERS

Computers and associated technologies are notorious in terms of the apprehension, sometimes even fear, they engender in people.

Question barrier: When machines will give the answer before they are asked the question.

A computer is the only machine that is built without a specific use in mind.

MAS

The trouble with computers is that they do what you tell them, not what you want.

D. Cohen

The computer is to the information industry roughly what the central power station is to the electrical industry.

Peter Drucker

Computers are unreliable but humans are even more unreliable.

Gilb

It is a waste of time and money to put something into a computer if all you're going to do is print it out.

Ian Carlaw

When a piece of machinery is given an upgrade, it performs better. When a computer system is given an upgrade, it means that it can now do the job for which it was purchased.

CONFIDENCE

They can because they think they can.

Virgil

Nothing is harder to win back than lost confidence.

They conquer who believe they can.

Ralph Waldo Emerson

If you have the confidence, anything is possible. I have the confidence.

A. Bond

A person who smiles in the face of adversity probably has a scapegoat.

CONSCIENCE

Conscience is the inner voice which warns us someone may be looking.

Conscience gets a lot of credit that belongs to cold feet.

All too often a clear conscience is merely the result of a bad memory.

CONSIDERATION

The friend and the horse; don't tire them.

Give me the ability to see good things in unexpected places and talents in unexpected people, and please give me the grace to tell them so.

Do not do to others what you would not like yourself.
Confucius

CONTEST

Pick battles big enough to matter, but small enough to win.
Price Pritchett, Ron Pound

Don't be so determined to win points when you ought to be working at not losing them. Club-level matches are not won. They're lost. Someone beats you not because they win more points than you but because you lose more points than them.

Patricia D. Cornwell

CONTROL

There must not only be control; it must be seen to be there.

There is no use worrying about things over which you have no control, and if you have control, you can do something about them instead of worrying.

Stanley C. Allyn

Never light a fire you can't put out.

Never open a door you can't lock behind you.

COOKING

If in doubt, add more wine.

In cooking, as in all arts, simplicity is the sign of perfection.

Curnonsky

CORRECTNESS

Argue about what is right – not about who is right.

MAS

What matters is being right; not being told you are.

The fact that people grant that you are right doesn't mean that you are.

Do what you believe to be correct.
Don't be afraid to trust your heart.

In these days of political correctness, one may no longer snigger. You are permitted only to snegro.

Eric Henry

COSTS

You don't pay for what a product is worth. You pay for the inefficiencies associated with the production of that product.

Sam Smith

ELIMINATION APPROACH

Not cost reduction or increased efficiency but elimination of expense. 'If it were not for what basic cause, could this cost be eliminated?' This avoids the tendency to justify the existence of an operation or a cost.

People today are chiefly concerned with the higher things in life – like prices.

R. Greer

Experience tells us that a thing of beauty is a great expense.

It costs nothing to guess, but to guess wrongly can be very costly indeed.

Definition of 'A builder's estimate':
A sum of money equal to half the final cost.

Neil Collins

The best things in life are expensive.

Get it into perspective. It's only money.

One man's wage rise is another man's price increase.

Harold Wilson

COURAGE

He that dares not venture must not complain of ill-luck.

You have to run very quickly if you have no courage.

True courage is to do without witnesses that which you are capable of doing before all the world.

La Rochefoucauld

Courage is not freedom from fear; it is being afraid and still going on.

Behold the turtle: he only makes progress when he sticks his neck out.

James B. Conant

The trapeze artist will attempt more daring feats if he has a safety net.

John Adams

True courage can be the courage to make one's choice.

It is so easy to be brave for someone else.

Don't be afraid to go out on a limb; that's where the fruit is.

If you have the courage to begin, you have the courage to succeed.

Boldness has genius, power and magic.

COWARDICE

In unanimity there is cowardice and uncritical thinking.

To know what is right, and not to do it, is the worst cowardice.

A coward is one who, in an emergency, thinks with his legs.

How comes it to pass, then, that we appear such cowards in reasoning, and are so afraid to stand the test of ridicule?
A. Cooper

He who fights and runs away, lives to fight another day.
Percy French

They came for the Jews, I didn't speak. They came for the Catholics and still I didn't speak. Finally, they came for me: there wasn't anyone left to speak.
Pastor Martin E. Niemoller

CREATIVITY

Inspiration soon dies and is with difficulty reborn, but ingenuity only sleeps and is easily awakened.
L. Stein

Myth no. 1: Creativity diminishes with age.
Dr P.W. Buffington

Myth no. 2: Creativity is always linked to intelligence.

Dr P.W. Buffington

Why aren't people more creative? The answer is best explained by the fact that creativity is drastically reduced by laziness. Clay's Conclusion sums it up best: 'Creativity is great; but plagiarism is faster.' A lot of people don't want to expend the energy; as a result, some people creatively produce very little. Creativity is a combination of intuitiveness, enthusiasm, flexibility, intelligence, independence and initiative. Anyone can have creative ideas, but trusting them and putting them into practice builds creative character.

Dr. P.W. Buffington

CRIME

Criminal activity is 1 per cent motivation and 99 per cent opportunity.

The French Riviera/Costa del Sol/wherever is a sunny place for shady people.

Somerset Maugham

Guns do not cause crimes, people cause crimes.

Nobody steals to do nice things.

CRITICISM

Persecution is the first law of society because it is always easier to suppress criticism than meet it.

Howard M. Jones

Censure is the tax a man pays to the public for being eminent.

J. Swift

Remember that no solution is a bad solution; there are only better, more creative solutions. Don't be too hasty to criticise.

Dr P.W. Buffington

Criticism spares the ravens and attacks the doves.

Juvenal

I love criticism, just so long as it's unqualified praise.

Noel Coward

No character, however upright, is a match for constantly reiterated attacks, however false.

Alexander Hamilton

What a terrific din there would be if we made as much noise when things go right as we do when things go wrong.

Kathleen Bromley

Criticism is something you can avoid by saying nothing, doing nothing and being nothing.

To criticise the incompetent is easy. It is more difficult to criticise the competent.

All of us could take a lesson from the weather; it pays no attention to criticism.

You can't please everybody. Don't let criticism worry you.

Robert Louis Stevenson

There is so much good in the worst of us, and so much bad in the best of us, that it hardly becomes any of us to talk about the rest of us.

Francis Lally

There is no wall with a surface so smooth, that if mud is thrown at it some will not stick.

MAS

CRITICS

But there are some commentators who have made their careers pointing to our difficulties, talking down our successes and telling business how to do its job. You know this kind of thing. You have heard it, too. Well let me say to these commentators: 'If you can do it better, you go and do just that.'

A critic is a man who teaches others how to run when he has no legs himself.

Only the man who is ready to help has the right to criticise.

One disapproving voice rings much louder than ten admiring ones.

Robert Schumann

It requires very little ability to find fault.
That is why there are so many critics.

A critic is a person who knows the way, but can't drive the car.

Kenneth Tynan

Critics are to authors what dogs are to lamp-posts.

Jeffrey Robinson

CUSTOMERS

CUSTOMER RELATIONSHIP

It is necessary to remind ourselves that we are working in a service industry and that all our jobs, in the final analysis, rest on giving our customers complete satisfaction and value for their money. Frankly, and I hope that you will agree with me, anyone who does not agree with the aforementioned principle or does not wish to serve the customer, has no right to work in this exciting business of ours.

Remembering who your customers are and committing yourself and your organisation to quality are simple steps that are all too often ignored. Simply put, handle every transaction as if you will have to live with that customer in a very small room for the rest of your life. The quest for quality is not a one-time challenge. It is a never-ending process that must be continuously refuelled and refined. We must, however, learn from our mistakes and take from our successes. The competition won't wait . . . will you?

Dr M. Mescon

Customers are not people with whom to argue or match wits.

Success is furthered if customers are treated as if you'll be in contact with them time and time again.

CUSTOMER SERVICE

Customers are the most important persons in our business.
Customers are not dependent on us – we are dependent on them.
Customers are not an interruption of our work – they are the purpose of it.
Customers are part of our business – not outsiders.
Customers do us a favour when they call – we are not doing them

a favour by serving them.
Customers deserve the most courteous and attentive treatment.
Customers are the life blood of this and every other business.

Customer dissatisfaction is the greatest failure of any business.

MAS

If we don't take care of the customer, somebody else will.

Customers are not statistics; customers are people.

DEATH

It takes more than guns to kill a man.

Joe Hill

Few persons want to stop living because of the cost.

Space travel is the only presently known way of leaving this
world without dying.

Col J.P. Stapp

I am ready to meet my Maker. Whether my Maker is prepared
for the great ordeal of meeting me is another matter.

Winston S. Churchill

Depend upon it, sir, when a man knows he is to be hanged in a
fortnight, it concentrates his mind wonderfully.

Samuel Johnson

To the recipient, death is always novel.

When you've buried the dead you go on living.

Cemeteries contain many indispensable people.

The dead live again when their friends talk about them.

Maeterunck

Time and education can cure ignorance.
There is no cure for death.

Morris West

Cowards die many times before their deaths; the valiant never taste death but once.

Death is an infinite sleep – without dreams.

Socrates

DECEPTION

If a man deceive me once, shame on him; if he deceive me twice, shame on me.

Youth and skill are no match for old age and treachery.

The easiest person to deceive is oneself. Whatever a man wants to believe is assumed to be true.

If I were two-faced, would I be wearing this one?

Abraham Lincoln

It is surprising how few people are willing to support the truth, and how many people are willing to accept the deceit.

DELAY

How does a project get to be a year late? One day at a time.

One of the most labour-saving inventions of today is tomorrow.

Delay is preferable to error.

Thomas Jefferson

Delay is the deadliest form of negation.

C. Northcote Parkinson

Recent research has tended to show that the Abominable No-Man is being replaced by the Prohibitive Procrastinator.

C. Northcote Parkinson

Slowly does it can be too slow.

Hold your tongue and keep your pen in your pocket until you know the full facts.

A friend enlightened me about the meaning of the word 'mañana'. He told me about a workman on his mother's ranch near La Paz, Mexico, whom he had berated for putting off a job for several weeks. As my friend's ire rose the man smiled and nodded sagaciously. 'You know, señor,' the unperturbed Mexican said, 'we have finally figured out what is wrong with you gringos. You think "mañana" means tomorrow. It does not mean tomorrow. It means "not today".'

Fred Hoctor

DELUSION

Years don't make a man wise – they simply make him older.

He was a legend in his own mind.

Jack Segal

Just make sure your reach doesn't exceed your grasp.

He was suffering from delusions of adequacy.

Conceit may puff a man up but it will never prop him up.

Ruskin

Honours are only epaulettes.

Richard Feynman

Being a politician is like being a baseball manager; you have to be smart enough to understand the game and dumb enough to think it's important.

Eugene McCarthy

Let the people be; don't open their eyes. Supposing you did, what would they see? Their misery! Leave their eyes closed and let them go on dreaming.

Nikos Kazantzakis

DEMOCRACY

The chief support of an autocracy is a standing army.
The chief support of a democracy is an educated people.

L.D. Cauffman

Man's capacity for justice makes democracy possible, but man's inclination to injustice makes democracy necessary.

R. Niebuhr

In a democracy, the opposition is not only tolerated as constitutional, but must be maintained because it is indispensable.

W. Lippmann

Democracy: In which you say what you like and do what you're told.

Democracy is the recurrent suspicion that more than half of the people are right more than half of the time.

E.B. White

Democracy is the worst form of government, except all these other forms that have been tried from time to time.

Winston S. Churchill

In a democracy even the losers have a vote.

Robert Field

Democracy is always a lot of trouble, tiresome to some people. Dictatorship is more orderly.

Jimmy Reid

Anyone who values freedom and democracy should fight whenever these values are threatened.

Mark Berent

Democracy does not guarantee equality of conditions; it only guarantees equality of opportunity.

Irving Kristol

DESIGN

The test of good design is 'Does it work?'

It's much easier to design something excessively complicated than to attain simplicity and elegance.

Peter Dron

Strategy has to be very simple. If you can't explain it to a seven-year-old, it ain't going to work.

Claes Hultman

DESPAIR

A great Scottish preacher has pointed out that the real profanity of man is not some swear words we use. Those words are more stupid than sinful. The most profane word we use, he said, is the word 'hopeless'. When you say a situation or a person is hopeless, you are slamming the door in the face of God.

Dr Charles L. Allen

The most despairing word in the English language is 'bored'. If you have life, you have hope and ambition. To be bored is to have thrown in the towel, to have quit, to have joined the ranks of the living dead. Justify the air that you breathe – be alive in every sense of the word.

MAS

I'm finished; I've got cancer of my career.

Sometimes I get the feeling that the whole world is against me, but deep down I know that's not true. Some of the smaller countries are neutral.

Robert Orben

DESTINY

Sow an act and you reap a habit.
Sow a habit and you reap a character.
Sow a character and you reap a destiny.

Charles Reade

We have nowhere else to go . . . this is all we have.

Margaret Mead

The bad thing about good things is that they come to an end, and the good thing about bad things is that they also end.

The reason lightning doesn't strike twice in the same place is that the same place isn't there the second time.

Willie Tyler

DETAILS

It is not possible for an executive to hold himself aloof from anything . . . success is the sum of detail.

Harold Firestone

You have told us all we can reasonably record. You have not told us whether your Service favours pins or paper clips because we haven't asked you and because you did not think the answer worth volunteering. There is a process on both sides of unconscious selection. Now it is always possible – and this is the worrying thing – it is always entirely possible that in a month or two we shall unexpectedly and quite desperately need to know about the pins and paper clips.

John Le Carré

53

DIET

I never met a calorie I didn't like.

Judy Hammer

I worry about scientists discovering that lettuce has been fattening all along . . .

Erma Bombeck

If you eat something and nobody sees you eat it, it has no calories.

Broken biscuits are calorie-free. The process of breaking causes calorie leakage.

Foods that have the same colour have the same calories.
For example, mushrooms and white chocolate.

Movie-related foods have no calories as they are part of the entire entertainment package and not part of your personal fuel. Some examples are popcorn, choc-ices, etc.

Things licked from knives and spoons have no calories if you are in the process of preparing food in the kitchen.

DIGNITY

Any work is great which lends dignity to a man.

If we are prepared to sacrifice dignity, we must also be prepared to sacrifice authority.

Never sacrifice your dignity.

Most things can be preserved in alcohol. Dignity, however, is not one of them.

DIPLOMACY

If you are a master, be sometimes blind: if a servant, sometimes deaf.

A retentive memory may be a good thing, but the ability to forget is the true token of greatness.

E. Hubbard

Diplomacy is possible only between established institutions, good or bad. In a revolutionary situation you cannot negotiate, only gamble.

Morris West

Not all politicians make good diplomats.

DISCIPLINE

The worst part about a lax education is that it does not instil a sense of discipline, high standards or competitive urgency in young people. Then they grow up and, of course, they don't expect discipline, high standards or competitive urgency from their children.

Make a point to do something each day that you don't want to.

Error is the discipline through which we advance.

Practise self-discipline. It is very hard to fall out of bed at 7.30am and get stuck in when there is no secretary and eager office staff depending on your arrival, but the prizes go to the men and women who can keep their own noses to the grindstone.

David Moreau

It is one thing to praise discipline, and another to submit to it.

Cervantes

DISCOVERIES

All great discoveries are made by men whose feelings run ahead of their thinking.

C.H. Parkhurst

I do not know what I may appear to the world, but to myself I seem to have been only like a boy playing on the seashore and diverting myself in now and then finding a smoother pebble or a prettier shell than ordinary, whilst the great ocean of truth lay all undiscovered before me.

Isaac Newton

What is wanted is not the will to believe, but the wish to find out, which is the exact opposite.

Bertrand Russell

The more original a discovery, the more obvious it seems afterwards.

Discovery consists of seeing what everybody has seen and thinking what nobody has thought.

Albert Szent-Gyorgyl

Each problem that I solved became a rule which served afterwards to solve other problems.

René Descartes

DISCRETION

What must be decided once and for all should be long considered.

Proof of intelligence on Mars is that they have not bothered to try to contact Earth.

DISCRIMINATION

The Army has carried the American ideal to its logical conclusion. Not only do they prohibit discrimination on the grounds of race, creed and colour, but also on ability.

Tom Lehrer

Since hate poisons the soul, do not cherish enmities or grudges. Avoid people who make you unhappy.

Robert Louis Stevenson

DISEASE

What physicians call a 'Waste-paper-basket diagnosis'.
You throw all the symptoms into a pot and then invent a disease.

Proper treatment will cure a cold in seven days, but left to itself, a cold will hang on for a week.

The virus of restlessness.

John Steinbeck

To chart the origin and course of a disease is one thing; to cure it is quite another.

Morris West

DISHONESTY

I have known a vast quantity of nonsense talked about bad men not looking you in the face. Don't trust that conventional idea. Dishonesty will stare honesty out of countenance, any day of the week, if there is anything to be got by it.

C. Dickens

Round numbers are usually false.

There is no greater fraud than a promise unfulfilled.

The greatest weapons of tyranny are silence and false report.

Morris West

DISILLUSIONMENT

Be not angry that you cannot make others as you wish them to be, since you cannot make yourself as you wish to be.

T.A. Kempis

Fair? My dear ...., since when has fairness been a criterion of conduct? Is God fair? Does he weep to see a child die of starvation? Why should we be fair?

58

Middle-age is that time of life when you can feel bad in the morning without having fun the night before.

M. Hamilton

By the time a man finds greener pastures, he can't climb the fence.

E. Boone

It's pretty hard to tell what does bring happiness; poverty and wealth have both failed.

Kim Hubbard

The age of chivalry has gone and one of computers and economists succeeded.

Anyone who believes there is fairness in this life is seriously misinformed.

Jack Kennedy

In a fit of self-righteous indignation based on no foundation of fact.

When our heart goes out of our work, life starts to lose its sparkle.

Price Pritchett, Ron Pound

The cynics are right nine times out of ten.

H.L. Mencken

DISINTEREST

In the ideal sense nothing is uninteresting; there are only uninterested people.

B. Atkinson

Men inevitably become indifferent to anything they do often.

The biggest reason for lack of knowledge is lack of interest.

The worst sin towards our fellow creatures is not to hate them, but to be indifferent to them; that's the essence of inhumanity.

George Bernard Shaw

I careth not for thy predicament.

Jack Segal

He exhibited dynamic lethargy.

We shall have to repent, not so much for the evil deeds of the wicked people as the appalling silence of the good people.

Martin Luther King

DISLIKE

Some callers can stay longer in an hour than others can in a week.

'Go home' the crowd shouted – and threw things.

Jack Segal

Anyone who hates children and dogs can't be all bad.

W.C. Fields

I like the game; I dislike some of the people with whom I have to play it.

Morris West

DISRESPECT

There is among the children a prevailing and increasing want of respect towards their elders, more especially towards their parents.

Helen Bosanquet

DISTORTION

Misinformation is as dangerous as loaded guns and a thousand times as hard to fight.

Barbara Amiel

It serves no purpose for society to avoid from being judgmental, and replacing values with information.

Barbara Amiel

He was a devious person. He never changed the rules, but he did move the goalposts – and did not tell anyone that he had done so.

MAS

Even good news is bad news if it's false.

Chinese saying

DISTRUST

A banker is a fellow who lends you his umbrella when the sun is shining and wants it back the minute it begins to rain.

Mark Twain

Strive for simplicity, but be willing to mistrust it.

Alfred North Whitehead

All fishermen are liars, except you and me . . . and I'm not so sure about you.

DIVORCE

If you made a list of reasons why any couple got married, and another list of the reasons for their divorce, you'd have a lot overlapping.

If divorce could be obtained from a slot machine, there would be no married people in the world.

Harold Wachtel

DOCTORS

Osteopath: One who rubs you up the right way.

A doctor is the only man without a guaranteed cure for a cold.

The patient I can help quickest is the desperate one who knows he's sick.

Morris West

A doctor who treats himself has a fool for a patient.

DREAMING

If we can dream it, we can do it.

Don't part with your illusions. When they are gone you may still exist but you have ceased to live.

Mark Twain

If you have built castles in the air your work is not wasted. Just put the foundations under them.

Why not at least try to realise your dream, the one that deep down you would truly love to achieve.

Michael Dell

There are some nightmares from which the only escape is to awaken.

Castles in the air – they are so easy to take refuge in; so easy to build too.

Ibsen

Men live by their illusions.

DRINKING

It is better to be a 'drunk' than an 'alcoholic'.
A drunk doesn't have to attend all those damn meetings.

I know a chap with a very serious drinking problem – he has no money for drinks.

T. April

Three glasses of wine can end a thousand disputes.

Total abstainers are right, but only drinkers know why.

Simon Carmiggelt

Brandy and water spoils two good things.

Charles Lamb

I must get out of these wet clothes and into a dry Martini.

Alexander Woollcott

The water was not fit to drink. To make it palatable, we had to add whiskey. By diligent effort, I learned to like it.

Winston S. Churchill

Being stoned on marijuana isn't very different from being stoned on gin.

Ralph Nader

You're not drunk if you can lie on the floor without holding on.

Dean Martin

Man differs from a machine in that he is seldom quiet when well oiled.

The wonderful love of a beautiful maid,
The love of a staunch, true man.
The love of a baby unafraid,
Have existed since time began.
But the greatest love, the love of loves,
Even greater than that of a brother,
Is the tender, passionate, infinite love
Of one drunken bum for another.

'You're ugly.'
'You're drunk.'
'But tomorrow I'll be sober.'

A woman once drove me to drink and I never had the courtesy to thank her.

W.C. Fields

You don't buy beer; you just lease it.

Bruce Wilson

They were behaving like a group of daft wee boys who'd had too many wine gums.

MAS

DRIVE

He has the deed half done, who has made a beginning.

Horace

Action will not take place of its own accord. It must be prodded, pushed and cajoled from people.

Motivation is what gets you started.
Habit is what keeps you going.

Jim Ryun

DUTY

Doing one's duty is not a thing one must expect from others only.

With many people, duty means something unpleasant that the other fellow should do.

EATING

A great crime against gastronomy is when people, without tasting their food, pile on salt and/or pepper!

Yvonne Arnaud

My doctor advised me to give up those intimate little dinners for two – unless I had one other person eating with me.

John Marshall

Those who warn of a population explosion picture a world with too many people and not enough food – like the average cocktail party.

Bill Vaughan

Some people eat as though they were fattening themselves for market.

E.W. Howe

A full belly makes a dull brain.

Benjamin Franklin

A shared meal is food for friendship.

Who you eat and drink with is more important than what you eat and drink.

Seneca

A cheerful face makes a feast of the simplest meal.

Canapes – dead things on toast.

Jack Segal

Take time to enjoy good food. It is the source of health.

I will not eat oysters. I want my food dead, not sick, not wounded, DEAD !

Woody Allen

Cheese – milk's leap towards immortality.

Clifton Fadiman

Great restaurants are, of course, nothing but Mouth Brothels. There is no point in going to them if one intends to keep one's belt buckled.

Frederic Raphael

As for butter versus margarine, I trust cows more than chemists.

Joan Gussow

The best number for a dinner party is two; myself and a damn good head waiter.

Nubar Gulbenkian

Custard: A detestable substance produced by a malevolent conspiracy between the hen, the cow and the cook.

Ambrose Bierce

At dinner one should eat wisely but not too well, and talk well but not too wisely.

Somerset Maugham

There is no sincerer love than the love of food.

George Bernard Shaw

ECONOMY

There's no economy in going to bed early to save candles if the result is twins.

Chinese proverb

There can be no economy where there is no efficiency.

Benjamin Disraeli

If all economists were laid end to end, they would not reach a conclusion.

George Bernard Shaw

EDUCATION

School and university teachers have little grasp of economics or the world of business. We still do not actually teach people how to think. Indeed, it has been said that a university education develops all of a person's attributes, including his stupidity.

Of course, it would cost money; but if you think education is expensive, try ignorance.

Derek Bok

I think the great danger in public education today is the fact that we have failed to see the difference between knowledge and wisdom. We train the head and let the heart run wild. We allow culture and character to walk miles apart, stuffing the head with mathematics and languages – leaving manners and morals out of the picture.

Dr T.H. Palmquist

University degrees are like false teeth. You would rather not be without them, but you don't advertise that you've got them.

An educated person usually knows where to go to find out about what he doesn't know.

Being educated means to prefer the best not only to the worst, but to the second best.

W.L. Phelps

What does education often do? It makes a straight cut ditch of a free meandering stream.

Henry David Thoreau

The yardstick for the success of an education system should be the quality of its graduates and their usefulness to the nation; the quantity of graduates is of small consequence.

MAS

Those students who gain least from university are not only those who do too little work but those who do too much and deny themselves the many other pleasures of university life.

Without an education, you are sentencing yourself to a lifetime of degradation and poverty.

Roosevelt Dorn

EFFICIENCY

Efficiency is a state of mind – not a battery of business machines.

Friden Ltd

The beginning of efficiency is orderliness.

It is a mistake to take fussiness for efficiency.

A team is like a nice clock – if just one piece is missing the clock is still beautiful, but doesn't work the same.

Ruud Gullit

EFFORT

You cannot climb the ladder of success with your hands in your pockets.

A man's life is interesting primarily when he has failed – I well know. For it's a sign that he tried to surpass himself.

G. Clemenceau

Are we making enough effort?
Are we achieving the necessary results?

Every big success is the result of an intense interest.

EMBARRASSMENT

Man is the only animal that blushes . . . or needs to.

Mark Twain

When she opens her mouth, it seems that this is only to change whichever foot was previously in there.

EMPLOYMENT

A corporation prefers to offer an executive job to a man who already has one, or doesn't immediately need one. The Company accepts you if you are already accepted. To obtain entry into paradise . . . you should be in a full state of grace.

Alan Harrington

A company is known by the men it keeps.

ENDEAVOUR

It is common sense to take a method and try it. If it fails, admit it frankly and try another. But above all, try something.

Franklin D. Roosevelt

Better to fail in attempting exquisite things than to succeed in the department of the utterly contemptible.

A. Macken

But always remember, it's only goals that count. No one remembers the good attempts or the near misses or the one that got away.

The impossible is often the untried.

Jim Goodwin

We all try – you succeed.

You will never know what you can do unless you attempt what you think you cannot do.

Cameron Quinn

Try, and you might. Don't, and you certainly won't.

ENEMIES

Only ever engage the enemy when you can be certain of victory. Make that a rule of your life.

Never hate your enemies – it affects your judgement.

Apropos the House of Commons, the story is told of the new Member looking across the Chamber at the serried ranks opposite and saying to an old hand: 'It's good to get a sight of the enemy at last.' 'No, no, dear boy,' said the veteran. 'They are not the enemy. They are your opponents. Your enemies are on this side of the House.'

The better is the enemy of the good.

The worst enemy of all is fear.

Morris West

Forgive your enemies, but never forget their names.

John F. Kennedy

Friends may come and go, but enemies accumulate.

Thomas Jones

My enemy's enemy is my friend.

ENGLISH LANGUAGE

There is a simple way to reduce swearing. Limit your use of profane words to nouns. Do not use such words as verbs, adjectives or adverbs. Very soon, swearing will become a rare event.

MAS

If something is described as being out of this world, the description 'unearthly' could be applied as easily as 'heavenly'.

MAS

A dictionary is the only place where 'success' comes before 'work'.

The English have no respect for their language, and will not teach their children to speak it.

George Bernard Shaw

It's not the time it takes to take the takes that takes the time; it's the time it takes between the takes that takes the time.

Steven Spielberg

The distinction between true and false appears to become increasingly blurred by the pollution of the language.

Arne Tiselius

Consider, we could spell 'fish' this way: GHOTI. The 'f' as in enough, the 'i' as in women, and the 'sh' as in fiction. With such peculiar rules to follow, no one should feel stupid about being a bad speller.

It's a strange world of language in which skating on thin ice can get you into hot water.

F.P. Jones

Exercise in punctuation:
John where David had had had had had had had had had was better.
John, where David had had 'had', had had 'had had'; 'had had' was better.

Whenever you read the message from a Chinese fortune cookie, try adding the words 'in bed' to the end of it. The results can be rather interesting.

Jim Baumgarten

The danger of misplaced punctuation can be disastrous: 'You must never think you are in this world solely for the purpose of making money' became in the report of a bishop's sermon, 'You must never think. You are in this world solely for the purpose of making money.'

ENJOYMENT

Surely, liking to do something is the first step towards doing it well.

Grief can take care of itself, but to get the full value of joy it must be shared.

Never run after your own hat – others will be delighted to do it; why spoil their fun?

Mark Twain

Don't put off for tomorrow what you can do today, because if you enjoy it today, you can do it again tomorrow. Also, if you don't do it today you may never get the chance to do it.

Enjoy life now. This is not a rehearsal.

Do the things you enjoy doing, but stay out of debt.

Robert Louis Stevenson

ENTHUSIASM

Enthusiasm is like fire; it needs both feeding and watching.

Enthusiasm for learning should be encouraged as much as possible. It is a rare trait.

What oil does for an engine, enthusiasm does for your work; it makes it go easily.

Whatever you do, work at it with all your heart.
Colossians 3:23

Nothing will dispel enthusiasm like a small admission fee.
Kim Hubbard

One ounce of keenness is worth a whole library of certificates.

A man can succeed at almost anything for which he has unlimited enthusiasm.
Charles M. Schwab

He lived life with the intensity of God giving Moses the Ten Commandments.
William Ronald Miller

ENVY

When a man says money can do everything, that settles it; he hasn't any.
E.W. Howe

Envy is a pain of mind that successful men cause their neighbours.
Onasander

Few shoes into which envious men would step indicate how hot and hurt are their wearer's feet.
H.S. Haskins

Watch what people are cynical about, and one can often discover what they lack, and, subconsciously, beneath their tough condescension, deeply wish they had.

H.E. Fosdick

Envy is a vice of the inadequate.

EPITAPHS

Inscription on the tombstone of a notorious hypochondriac: 'See!'

M. Jones

If I should die before I wake, all my bone and sinew take.
Put me in the compost pile, to decompose me for a while.
Worms, water, sun, will have their way, returning me to
   common clay.
All that I am will feed the trees, and little fishes in the seas.
When radishes and corn you munch, you may be having me for
   lunch,
And then excrete me with a grin,
Chuckling 'There goes Lee again.'

Lee Hays

It is so soon that I am done for,
I wonder what I was begun for.

Of this bad world the loveliest and the best
Has smiled and said Goodnight and gone to rest.
Hilaire Belloc, on the death of a lady

Epitaph on tombstone
   Stay stranger, see where I lie.
   As you are now so once was I.

And as I am so shall you be.
Prepare for death, and follow me.
Added by visitor:
    To follow you I'm quite content,
    But damned if I know which way you went.

When you go home, tell them of us and say,
For your tomorrow, we gave our today.

The Kohima Epitaph

If I should go before the rest of you
Break not a flower nor inscribe a stone
Nor when I'm gone – speak in a Sunday voice,
But be the usual selves that I have known.
Weep if you must; parting is hell
But life goes on – so smile as well.

ESCAPISM

A grouch escapes so many little annoyances that it almost pays to
be one.

K. Hubbard

No problem is so big or so complicated that it can't be run away
from.

Charles Schulz

People in specialised industries or in the professions are often
put in an embarrassing position during some social meeting by
someone asking advice that is really a request for a professional
opinion. If you are subjected to this, and you wish to stop the
process without being rude, churlish or giving offence, all that
you have to do is ask one question: 'Is this a consultation?'

MAS

You can't keep running away from the truth; the world just isn't big enough.

EVIL

The only thing necessary for the triumph of evil is for good men to do nothing.

Edmund Burke

Slander injures three – the speaker, the spoken to, and the spoken of.

Evil is easily acquired – good is not.

Chinese proverb

Cruelty must be whitewashed by a moral excuse, and pretence of reluctance.

George Bernard Shaw

Evils can be created much quicker than they can be cured.

Winston S. Churchill

When choosing between two evils, I always like to try the one I've never tried before.

Mae West

EXAGGERATION

Exaggeration is the cheapest indulgence.

Exaggeration is the lie of honest people.

There are people so addicted to exaggeration that they can't tell the truth without lying.

Josh Billings

Don't say a thing's impossible when it is only difficult.

He ascribes superlativity to every mediocrity in his possession.

William Ronald Miller

EXCESS

Money, food and sex; only too much is enough.

Arthur Yaffy

As is the case with a light bulb, the man who is always switched on is the first to burn out.

All sunshine makes a desert.

Moderation is a fatal thing. Nothing succeeds like excess.

Oscar Wilde

I have always noticed that whenever a radical takes to imperialism, he catches it in a very acute form.

Winston S. Churchill

Over-rich, over-privileged and far too easily bored.

EXCUSES

What I want are results, not excuses.

Don't tell me why a proposed scheme won't succeed.
Tell me what other scheme will succeed.

Excuses are easily found – but the wise man looks for reasons.

Handy guide to NEGATIVE THINKING
It's been done this way for years – why change? . . .That's been
tried before . . . Our business is different . . .We'll come back to
it later . . . It leaves me cold . . . Let's think about it some more
. . . This isn't the right time for it . . . We can't hold up production for that . . . Cost is not important – just get it out the
back door . . . We can't help it; it's policy . . . We don't have
enough time . . .We don't do it that way . . . It costs too much . . .
That's not my responsibility . . . No one else knows as much
about it as we do.

It's easy to find excuses for losing.

You are saying that these are only teething troubles and that all
will be well once the teething troubles are over? Sir, you are
wrong. These aren't teething troubles. They aren't even a touch
of gout. It's a car crash and the fatalities have yet to be counted.
Susannah Herbert

I'm sorry the show has been delayed, but the drummer has been
taken suddenly drunk.
Ronnie Scott

EXPECTATION

Be wary of extremes: the green and the overripe fruit cause the
worst pain.

Those who plant thorns must not expect to pluck roses.

I set a high standard for myself and I expect others to do the same. I cannot tolerate laziness, sloppiness or excuses for inefficiency. The people who work under me know this. If they cannot do the job then they are out.

Blessed is he who expecteth nothing, for he shall not be disappointed.

Things may come to those who wait, but only the things left behind by those who hustle.

Abraham Lincoln

EXPEDIENCY

Always suggest an alternative, especially if you know it's one that won't suit the particular bill.

If you are losing a tug-of-war with a tiger, give him the rope before he gets to your arm. You can always buy a new rope.

Max Gunther

EXPERIENCE

Some think they have gained experience simply by growing old.

An optimist is a man who hasn't had much experience.

D. Marquis

Most people are happier buying experience than paying for advice.

Experience is a marvellous thing. It enables you to recognise a mistake whenever you make it again.

Experience is a great teacher.
Too often it is also a great preacher.

You are correct when you say that he's only got five years' experience and you've got twelve years' experience. The reason he got the job is that he's got five years' experience whereas you've got one year's experience twelve times over.

Experience is not what happens to a man. It is what a man does with what has happened to him.

EXPERTS

Definition of an expert: A man who comes from more than 20 miles away.

An expert is a person who avoids the small errors as he sweeps on to the grand fallacy.

B. Stolberg

An expert is a lecturer from out of town, with slides.

Jim Baumgarten

FACTS

Facts that have to be faced are so often ugly.

If the facts conflict with your expectations, always believe the facts.

Facts do not cease to exist because they are ignored.

Aldous Huxley

Comment is free but facts are sacred.

C.P. Scott

You can't share an exclusive.

Facts speak louder than statistics.

Don't confuse me with facts – my mind is made up.

Every man has a right to his own opinion, but no man has a right to be wrong in his facts.

Bernard M. Baruch

Every problem has a solution, and if there is no solution then it is a fact and not a problem. We must then learn to live with that fact.

MAS

Facts are stubborn things.

FAILURE

Success has many shareholders but failure is the sole property of the people responsible.

When you're down you are not necessarily a failure. It's staying down that makes you a failure.

A man surprised is half beaten.

Of the fallen tree, everybody makes firewood.

Failures always tell you how hard they tried.

There are two kinds of men who never amount to much – those who cannot do what they are told, and those who can do nothing else.

I cannot give you the formula for success, but I can give you the formula for failure which is 'Try to please everybody.'

A bunch of has-beens and never-will-bes.

Woe unto him who is alone when he falleth, for he hath not another to help him.

'Our only "crime" is that we failed.'
'That is the only crime that matters.'

As far as this project is concerned, failure is not an option.

Failure begins when you stop trying to succeed.

Remember this: when you are through changing, you're through.

Failure is often the line of least persistence.

Zig Zagler

Glory is fleeting, but obscurity is forever.

Napoleon Bonaparte

Being a failure isn't as easy as it looks.

FAITH

All the strength and force of a man comes from his faith in things unseen. He who believes is strong; he who doubts is weak. Strong convictions precede great actions. The man strongly possessed of an idea is the master of all who are uncertain or wavering. Clear, deep, living convictions rule the world.

J.F. Clarke

What I admire about Columbus is not his having discovered a new world, but his having gone to search for it on the faith of an opinion.

F. Benson

Solfidian: One who holds that faith alone is necessary for justification.

Faith lies in the heart; not in the knees.

FALLIBILITY

The cemeteries are full of people who thought that the world couldn't get along without them.

David Lipton

Nothing is so strong that it will not break.

It's nice to know that you're fallible sometimes.

Sheila J. Cooper

Perfect solutions of our difficulties are not to be looked for in an imperfect world.

Winston S. Churchill

FAMILY

One often finds that the best thing about distant relations is the distance.

The biggest problem you face at this time of year is to convince the kids that you're Father Christmas and your wife that you aren't.

I and my brother against our cousin;
I and my cousin against the world.

Arabic saying

Don't judge people by their relatives.

FASHION

For an idea ever to be fashionable is ominous, since it must afterwards be always old-fashioned.

G. Santayana

Fashion is the heaviest taxation we have to pay.

She was spending money like it was going out of fashion.

Beware of all enterprises that require new clothes.

H.D. Thoreau

FATE

The world is made of stairs – and there are those people who go up and those who go down.

The day my ship comes in I'll probably be at the railway station.

Abel Walport

Most of us get what we deserve, but only the successful will admit it.

FAULT

The greatest of all faults is to be conscious of none.

Thomas Carlyle

One should allow everyone three faults. If we make that allowance, we find that the rest is surprisingly nice.

In any given miscalculation, the fault will never be placed if more than one person is involved.

Merle P. Martin

He is lifeless that is faultless.

FEAR

Do not beware of dog. Beware of owner of dog.

A good scare is worth more to a man than good advice.

The fear of a threat to his personal security is at the root of every person's violence and hatred.

Tennessee Williams

Fear defeats more men than any other one thing in the world.

The insecurity that the British class system inflicts upon those not born into the upper echelons.

It's not contemptible to be afraid.

Dr S. Lenk

Fear is a habit; I am not afraid.

Fear – that is the other guy's problem.

It is better to be feared than loved, if you cannot be both.

Machiavelli

Fear is like a darkroom where little doubts get developed.

David Watt

FEELINGS

Intuition is genius when it works; but plain stupidity when it doesn't.

Mixed emotions is being middle-aged and suddenly realising you'll never be a has-been.

F.O. Walsh

An idealist is someone who thinks with the heart.

Heaven and Hell are not places – they are feelings.

He/she has a capacity for insensitivity paralleled only by Attila the Hun.

Scott Hughes

The most difficult sets of feelings for a person to handle are those brought on by a death, divorce, or moving house.

FINANCE

Don't fund too much or else the entrepreneurs get discouraged.

If you don't understand a complicated financial idea it does not necessarily follow that you're stupid. The notion itself may be fundamentally flawed.

Donald Trelford

FORESIGHT

You can't be sure of anything these days. Just think of all the mothers who, 20 years ago, had their daughters vaccinated in places they thought wouldn't show.

V. Guffey

It is wise to look ahead, but foolish to look further than you can see.

Winston S. Churchill

You can never plan the future by the past.

Edmund Burke

It is a mistake to look too far ahead. Only one link in the chain of destiny can be handled at a time.

Winston S. Churchill

Remember the toes you stand on today may be attached to the legs that support the arse you have to kiss tomorrow.

Watt Nicoll

FORGIVENESS

If you forgive people enough you belong to them, and they to you, whether either person likes it or not – squatter's rights of the heart.

James Hilton

To err is human; to forgive is not my policy.

Sam Chisholm

It is easier to beg forgiveness than to ask for permission.

'Forgive me, but . . . ' is invariably the prelude to something quite unforgivable.

Without forgiveness revenge would be rampant, the spiral of violence in the world would outpace even its present speed and our hearts would be corroded by festering resentment or by an anger and hatred that never abates.

William Wolff

The stupid neither forgive nor forget, and the naive forgive and forget. However, the wise forgive but do not forget.

Thomas Szasz

Forgive. Grudges are too heavy to carry around.

Price Pritchett, Ron Pound

FREEDOM

Freedom is not worth having if it does not connote freedom to err.

Gandhi

A free life is the only life worthy of a human being. That which is not free is not responsible, and that which is not responsible is not moral. In other words, freedom is the condition of morality.

T. Davidson

Freedom is nothing else but the chance to do better.

Camus

With freedom comes responsibility; that is why so many are frightened by it.

George Bernard Shaw

Freedom is just another word for 'nothing left to lose'.

Freedom is a state of mind and not of being.

No one is really free while others are oppressed.

Freedom is defended by the shield of readiness.

You pass this way but once. There is no normal; there is not such a thing as normal. There's you and the rest. There's now and there's forever. Do as you damn well please.

Billy Connolly

FRIENDSHIP

The richest man is the one with the most powerful friends.

Friendship is almost always the union of a part of one mind with a part of another; people are friends in spots.

G. Santayana

Take time to be friendly – it is the road to happiness.

Before borrowing money from a friend, decide which you need more.

A real friend is like bread and wine – a blessing.

Small presents keep a friendship alive.

Speaking to a good friend is the same as thinking aloud.

A friend is one who knows everything about you – and still likes you.

I look upon every day to be lost, in which I do not make a new acquaintance.

Samuel Johnson

A faithful friend is the medicine of life.

Apocrypha 6:16

Friendships are far more easy to build and less costly than battleships . . . and are far more powerful.

Sir Harry Lauder

There is no such thing as strangers. They're only friends you haven't met yet.

Please remember, I am not the enemy.

I am holding your hand. If, at any stage, I cease to be holding your hand it is because you have chosen to take your hand away. Please don't ever do that.

MAS

Prosperity makes friends; adversity tests them.

Forsake not an old friend, for the new is not comparable to him. A new friend is as new wine; when it is old, thou shalt drink it with pleasure.

Friends are like melons; to find a good one you must try a hundred.

Claude Mermet

Show me your friends, and I will tell you who you are.

Trevor McDonald

Don't let a little dispute injure a great friendship.

FUTURE

Today's man is a kind of technological Adam, standing on the threshold of a new world of millions of discoveries. Each year from now on will see more technological change than formerly took place in a generation.

J.L. Powell

The future is a race between education and catastrophe.

H.G. Wells

Never look back. The past is gone, never to return. Any and all thoughts must be for today, or for the future. These you can attempt to influence. Nobody can change the past.

The future is unlimited as long as man cares for mankind.

Roy Hickman

Part of our history perishes when someone dies, but part of our future is lost for ever when a young person dies.

A hundred years from now it will not matter what my bank account was, the sort of house I lived in or the kind of car I drove . . . but the world may be different because I was important in the life of a child.

Plan for the future – because that's where you're going to spend the rest of your life.

Henry Ford

When we fear for the future, we turn to someone who shouts loudest that he has the answers.

Robert Andrews

You just can't build a decent argument for giving in to fear of the future. All it amounts to is borrowing trouble.

Price Pritchett, Ron Pound

We cannot forget the past nor should we, but let us concentrate on the future.

Chaim Bermant

If you want to make God really laugh, start to plan for your future.

The best way to predict the future is to invent it.

Alan Kay

Tomorrow is promised to no one.

GAMES

I support two teams: Scotland, and whoever's playing England.

Donald Cameron

Baseball has the great advantage over cricket of being sooner ended.

George Bernard Shaw

If swimming is good for the figure, what about the whale?

In a game of tennis, if you can't immediately call the ball 'Out' then it must be 'In'.

Lew Hoad

Games are for winning or losing. Draws are meaningless.

Sports serve society by providing vivid examples of excellence, as well as providing pastime and pleasure.

Life's a game, but golf (or whatever) is serious.

In competition, nothing is less important than the score at half-time.

Fishing is much more than casting and retrieving and playing your catch. It's the wind in your face, and the sound of wakening

birds as the sun peeks over the horizon. It's discovering the magic in each new place and unlocking the mysteries that lurk there, both above and below the surface.

Serious sport has nothing to do with fair play. It is bound up with jealousy, boastfulness and disregard of all the rules.

George Orwell

During the game, there was a small outbreak of tennis.

MAS

GARDENS

As is the gardener, so is the garden.

T. Fuller

Many children enjoy seeing flowers come up – mostly by the roots.

Edible landscaping . . . using the garden to grow only that which can be eaten.

Bernard Hammer

The ancient Greeks simplified their conception of the fabric of their world by sub-dividing everything into Earth, Air, Fire and Water. Modern people could simplify their attitude towards gardens and gardening by classifying all growing things as Trees, Grass, Flowers or Weeds.

MAS

The easiest thing to grow in a garden is tired.

GENEROSITY

Lavishness is not generosity.

People are very generous with what costs them nothing.

The way you give your gift matters more than what you give.

Too much generosity breeds contempt, and not respect.

You can only share by giving away.

GENIUS

The function of genius is not to give new answers, but to pose new questions which time and mediocrity can resolve.

H.R. Trevor-Roper

I'm not a genius; but I'm a terrific package of experience.

It's no good having a spark of genius if you suffer from ignition trouble.

A doorman is a genius who can open the door of your car with one hand, help you in with the other, and still have one left for the tip.

D. Kilgallen

Genius is 1 per cent inspiration and 99 per cent perspiration.

Thomas Edison

Mediocrity knows nothing higher than itself, but talent immediately recognises genius.

Common sense is genius dressed in its working clothes.

Ralph Waldo Emerson

When a true genius comes among you, by this sign shall you know him; the dunces will be in confederacy against him.

Swift

GOD

I am always humbled by the infinite ingenuity of the Lord who can make a red barn cast a black shadow.

E.B. White

A baby is God's opinion that the world should go on.

God can't be everywhere – that's why he invented mothers.

God's work made a hopeful beginning,
But man spoiled his chances by sinning.
We hope that this story
Will end in God's glory,
But at present the other side's winning.

Goldfish are convinced there must be a God; how else does the water get changed?

If you talk to God, you are praying.
If God talks to you, then you have schizophrenia.

Thomas Szasz

GOLF

It is almost impossible to remember how tragic a place the world is when one is playing golf.

R. Lynd

The trouble with my golf game is that I stand too close to the ball after I've hit it.

Jack Benny

Some people play golf religiously – every Sunday.

D. Stevens

It's not that I really cheat at golf. I play for my health, and a low score helps me feel better.

R. Wilson

Handicapped golfer: One who is playing with his boss.

Golf is a good walk spoiled.

Nevertheless, it is well that we still retain a sense of relativity. In Africa, the natives have the custom of beating the ground with clubs and uttering blood-curdling yells. Anthropologists call this a form of self-expression. In Europe, we call it golf.

Golf rule number one: The ball should travel further than the divot.

Golf is deceptively simple and endlessly complicated. It satisfies the soul and frustrates the intellect. It is, at the same time, rewarding and maddening – it is without a doubt the greatest game mankind has ever invented.

GRATITUDE

Everybody's heart is open, you know, when they have recently escaped from severe pain, or are recovering the blessing of health.

J. Austen

Gratitude is the hardest of all emotions to express. There is no word capable of conveying all that one feels. Until we reach a world where thoughts can be adequately expressed in words, 'Thank you' will have to do.

A.P. Gouthey

I am so grateful for what has happened. I give thanks to the Gods of the Gods that our Gods pray to.

GREED

It is partly to avoid consciousness of greed that we prefer to associate with those who are at least as greedy as ourselves. Those who consume much less are a reproach.

C.H. Cooley

Those who want much are always much in need.

Horace

Everybody wants something for nothing.

Great food is like great sex. The more you have, the more you want.

Nobody gets to have their cake and to eat it.

Egoist: Yours belongs to me and mine belongs to nobody.

The selfish spirit of commerce knows no country and feels no passion or principle but that of gain.

Thomas Jefferson

There is enough in this world for everyone's need, but not enough for everyone's greed.

Gandhi

HAPPINESS

It is not how much we have, but how much we enjoy, that makes happiness.

Everything is funny as long as it is happening to somebody else.

Will Rogers

Happiness is watching a snow-plough cover a police car.

J. Davidson

To be happy at home is the ultimate result of all ambition.

The secret of happiness is to admire without desiring.

Happiness is an intermediate station between too little and too much.

My creed is this: happiness is the only good. The place to be happy is here. The time to be happy is now. The way to be happy is to help to make others so.

Cherish all your happy moments.
They make a fine cushion for old age.

Happiness isn't something you experience; it's something you remember.

Oscar Levant

With regard to a boat and a horse, the second happiest day is when you buy it. The happiest day is when you sell it.

Happiness is a yesterday thing.

Spike Milligan

Happiness is easy to talk; it is not easy to live.

Happiness is a gentle stirring of the soul.

Aristotle

Happy is the person who can say: 'Tomorrow do your worst, for I have lived today.'

Richard Brown

HEALTH

Halitosis is better than no breath at all.

Two things bad for the heart: running up stairs and running down people.

Good health isn't everything but without it everything counts for nothing.

The only way to keep your health is to eat what you don't want, drink what you don't like and do what you'd rather not.

Mark Twain

One of the symptoms of an approaching nervous breakdown is the belief that one's work is terribly important.

Bertrand Russell

HELL

It will be a cold day in Hell when . . .

The most prominent place in Hell is reserved for those who are neutral on the great issues of life.

Hell is empty and all the devils are here.

William Shakespeare (The Tempest)

Hell hath no limits, nor is it circumscribed in one place, for where we are is Hell, and where Hell is there must we ever be.

Christopher Marlowe

I never give them Hell. I just tell the truth and they think it's Hell.

Harry S. Truman

HELPLESSNESS

The needy are the last to receive help. They have no priority and they lack the ability to relieve their own suffering.

HINDSIGHT

I've got perfect vision: 20/20 hindsight.

No matter what you do, someone always knew you would.

Hindsight is a great educator.

HISTORY

One reason that history repeats itself is that so many people were not listening the first time.

Margaret Hussey

After you've heard two eye-witness accounts of a car accident you begin to wonder about history.

R. Greer

History is always repeating itself, but each time the price goes up.

The so-called lessons of history are, for the most part, the rationalisations of the victors.

History is written by the survivors.

Max Lerner

History belongs to the victors.

Peter Simple

A fundamental lesson of history is never appease an aggressor.

HONESTY

Has any reader ever found perfect accuracy in the newspaper account of any event of which he himself had inside knowledge?

E.V. Lucas

No one will go astray if the path is straight and narrow.

Honesty pays, but it doesn't seem to pay enough to suit some people.

F.M. Hubbard

Nothing astonishes men so much as common sense and plain dealing.

Ralph Waldo Emerson

All men profess honesty as long as they can. To believe all men honest would be folly. To believe none so is something worse.

John Quincy Adams

The only time you knew he was telling the truth was if the story did not present him favourably. He told very few such stories.

William Ronald Miller

'To tell you the truth . . .' is invariably the prelude to some fabrication.

It is difficult but not impossible to conduct strictly honest business.

It is a fine thing to be honest, but it is also very important to be right.

Winston S. Churchill

HOPE

Where there is no hope there can be no endeavour.

On the whole, I think we shall survive . . . The outlook is as bad as it has ever been, but thinking people realise that, and therein lies hope of its getting better.

J. Nehru

An appeaser is one who feeds a crocodile – hoping it will eat him last.

Winston S. Churchill

Remember, the tide turns at low water, as well as at high.

Lady to bank teller: 'I'd like to open a joint account with someone who has lots of money.'

H. Courtney

From your mouth to God's ears.

In the kingdom of hope there is no such season as winter.

Hope is a more powerful weapon than fear.

The only hope of the doomed is not to hope for safety.

Virgil

HOPELESSNESS

Desperation is a man who shaves before weighing himself on the bathroom scales.

R.E. Dorsey

The frontier jury returned a verdict of 'Suicide' on the man armed with a revolver who opened fire at a range of fifty yards upon a man armed with a rifle.

He started off badly and then fell away.

He reminds me very much of a gyroscope – always spinning around at a frantic pace, but not really going anywhere.

He has reached rock bottom, and has started to dig.

'If' is a two letter word for 'futility'.

Louis Phillips

HOUSING

There are plenty of ruined buildings in the world but not ruined stones. We have all we need to rebuild.

A comfortable house is a great source of happiness.

No house should ever be on any hill or on anything. It should be of the hill, belonging to it.

Frank Lloyd Wright

You can build a house, but a home must grow.

Multi-storey blocks are just filing cabinets for people.

Jimmy Reid

Home is where the heart is.

Anywhere I hang my hat is home.

The only difference between a prison and a fortress is that the fortress doors lock from the inside.

HUMILITY

Humility is the first of all virtues – for other people.

Oliver Wendell Holmes

Modesty is a vastly overrated virtue.

J.K. Galbraith

There are plenty of butterflies who deny they were once caterpillars.

Express a mean opinion of yourself occasionally; it will show your friends that you know how to tell the truth.

Ed Howe

Better to go back than go wrong.

It is my privilege to lay a stone on the cairn of this man's memory.

When I walk through the hospital and see children in wheel-chairs, children with no eyes or no arms and I'm in there for this little back problem and complaining that it hurts when I play, I realise just how small tennis is.

Steffi Graff

Eating words has never given me indigestion.

Winston S. Churchill

'He's very modest.'
'Absolutely true. But then he does have a lot to be modest about.'

Winston S. Churchill

HUNGER

Hunger does not breed reform; it breeds madness, and all the ugly distempers that make an ordered life impossible.

Woodrow Wilson

Real poor is hungry poor.

Kirk Douglas

Bread is an emotive substance. Shortage of it has traditionally been a sign of dangerous irritation among those prone to riot.

'What is your favourite dish, grandad?'
'All of them, my son. It's a great sin to say that this is good and that is bad.'
'Why? Can't we make a choice?'
'No, of course we can't.'
'Why not?'
'Because there are people who are hungry.'

Nikos Kazantzakis

There are people in the world so hungry that God cannot appear to them except in the form of bread.

Gandhi

HUSBANDS

Whenever I meet a man who would make a good husband, he is.

Susan Oliver

A husband is a bachelor whose luck has failed.

Lady Astor: 'If you were my husband, I'd poison your coffee.'
Winston Churchill: 'If you were my wife, I'd drink it.'

If all bridegrooms are gallant, where do thoughtless husbands come from?

Marrying a man is like buying something you've been admiring for a long time in a shop window. You may love it when you get it home, but it doesn't always go with everything.

A husband is what is left of the lover after the nerve has been extracted.

Helen Rowland

IDEAS

Don't start vast projects with half-vast ideas.

There is nothing more dangerous than a big idea in a little head.

Give employees awards for ideas that are worth trying, even if they don't always work out.

Michael Dell

A successful idea is a greater monument than a cathedral.

Wisdom is not a monopoly; I need someone to bounce ideas off.

Naim Attalah

IDLENESS

The man called 'theory', because he never worked.

He is not only idle who does nothing, but he is idle who might be better employed.

Socrates

Doing nothing on holiday is the same activity as loafing at home.

It is a terrible burden, having nothing to do.

Boileau

IGNORANCE

Ignorance is a voluntary misfortune.

He has remembered everything . . . and learned nothing.

The thing that doesn't fit is the most interesting.

Richard Feynman

I don't feel frightened by not knowing things.

Richard Feynman

The image of Glasgow as a city of foul-mouthed, bottle-throwing people is a travesty, just a product of southern ignorance.

Terry Butcher

Of all human lamentations, without doubt the most common is 'If only I had known.'

Ignorance can be remedied.

When plumbing the depths of his knowledge, you do not need a submarine. A snorkel is quite sufficient.

His ignorance is encyclopaedic.

Abba Eban

ILL-GRACE

Saying 'Sorry' can never excuse a deliberate action.

To remind the man of the good turns you have done him is very much like a reproach.

Demosthenes

The nasty taste of the meaninglessness of the forced apology.

IMAGE

Every man has a lurking wish to appear considerable in his native place.

Samuel Johnson

Every man has two faces – one for the home and one for the outside world.

Hermy Jankel

IMAGINATION

Imagination is the eye of the soul.

Joseph Joubert

Imagination is more important than knowledge.

Albert Einstein

I decided that I must first understand more or less how the answer probably looks. With this in mind, I can then go on working on the problem in the hope that in the future, this rough understanding can be refined.

Richard Feynman

IMPOSSIBILITY

An impossible sentence to write: 'The farmer is sowing and his wife is sewing. Both are S_WING.'

MAS

You can change a river's course but you can't turn it back to its source.

IMPROVEMENT

Makes better; not cures.

To change and to improve are two different things.

Not getting older, getting better.

It is not everything that has changed for the better.

If you want a better world, get busy on your own little corner.

Take the best and make it better.

Henry Royce

Is there anything so perfect that it cannot be improved?

INABILITY

Those who can, do; those who can't, teach.

In any hierarchy every employee tends to rise to his level of incompetence. In time, every post tends to be occupied by an employee who is incompetent to carry out its duties.

Dr Laurence J. Peter

Rational thought is hard work. It may be that my own resources are not abundant, but I have found rational thought a considerable strain. The great civil servant Sir John Anderson did not believe that anyone could really concentrate for more than twenty minutes at a time. So much for all those ten-hour- a-day thinkers. How often has one heard people say 'I can't get down to work because of those phone calls and visitors I get.' But could they have survived without those welcome distractions? Were they in fact capable of concentrating at all? Maybe those visitors and phone calls were the perfect alibi for inability.

Unable to distinguish between opinion and fact.

The general tendency of things throughout the world is to render mediocrity the ascendant power among mankind.

John Stuart Mill

INEVITABILITY

He that rides on a tiger can never dismount.

The only way to conciliate a tiger is to allow yourself to be eaten.

Konrad Adenauer

People always get what they ask for; the only trouble is that they never know, until they get it, what it actually is that they have asked for.

Aldous Huxley

If you play with a thing long enough, it will break.

William J. Abercrombie

Modern man doesn't seem to realise that newer generations will follow him.

As I sat musing one day,
Sad and lonely and without a friend,
From out of the gloom a voice came to me saying
'Cheer up, things could be worse.'
So I cheered up, and sure enough, things got worse.

Nothing is so bad that it does not have a good side, and nothing is so good that there isn't a risk somewhere.

Brian Meek

INFERIORITY

No one can make you feel inferior without your consent.

Eleanor Roosevelt

No one can give you an inferiority complex without your own contribution.

INGRATITUDE

Human bones are not filled with red marrow, they are filled with black ingratitude.

Dr Myer S. Green

It is another's fault if he be ungrateful, but it is mine if I do not give. To find one thankful man I will oblige a great many that are not so.

Seneca

INJUSTICE

To them that have shall be given; from them that have not shall be taken away.

Abel Walport

No majority ever gave a minority a fair share.

Injustice anywhere is a threat to justice everywhere.

Martin Luther King

There is no justice if you are poor.
People care only about what happens to important persons.

INSTABILITY

We are not so much steering a course as drifting with the tides of circumstance. We are unduly subject to the influence of external and internal forces.

Causes do not endure.

INSULTS

Insults are the arguments for those who are in the wrong.

A well-educated person will never insult you – the rest can't, anyway.

To say (whomsoever) is grey is being rude to porridge.
Sir Nicholas Fairbairn

That is precisely the reaction I would have expected from a man of your obvious limitations.

They are quite a couple: she uglies for the West of Scotland and he bores for Glasgow.
Dan Carlaw

His men would follow him anywhere, but only out of curiosity.

This man is depriving a village somewhere of an idiot.

When was your lobotomy? I would have sent flowers.
Patricia D. Cornwell

INTEGRITY

Always act as if your acts were seen.

Live that you wouldn't be ashamed to sell the family parrot to the town gossip.

Honour, like life, once lost is never recovered.

Good journalists try to make their paper, and not themselves, interesting.

Be big enough to do the right thing.

INTELLIGENCE

Intelligent people never listen and the stupid never speak.
Oscar Wilde

You can always spot a well-informed, intelligent man. His views are the same as yours.

Don't work hard. Work smarter.

INTOLERANCE

People who won't suffer fools gladly must find solitude bearable.

We seem to have grown less tolerant of frustration of any kind and someone has to be blamed for everything.

He couldn't be changed, couldn't be argued with, and could not have his mind touched in any way. He was a closed shop, and the management had gone home.

Ian Rankin

A split-second could be defined as the time between the lights turning green and the car behind you sounding its horn.

INVOLVEMENT

If you don't like beans, you shouldn't have opened the tin.

There is no substitute for active participation.

MAS

Involvement with people is always a very delicate thing – it requires real maturity to become involved and not get all messed up.

Bernard Cooke

Whenever I hear anyone arguing for slavery, I feel a strong impulse to see it tried on him personally.

Abraham Lincoln

If you don't want to get your hands dirty, don't play in the mud.

IRRESPONSIBILITY

Lazy man work twice; stingy man pay twice.

If we want to rebuild the institutions of civil society we – the citizenry – have to do it ourselves. Whingeing about Westminster and Whitehall will not get us very far.

Robert Whelan

It's very easy to spend other people's money.

It is so often true that engineers, scientists and systems designers are so intent and absorbed in whatever it is that they are trying to achieve that they never give any thought beforehand to what might be the consequences of what they plan to invent. This is amoral.

Colin Forbes

There's no use running if you're on the wrong road.

I'm living so far beyond my income that we may almost be said to be living apart.

E.E. Cummings

JEWISH PEOPLE

Jewish people aren't an audience; they're competition.

While the world stood by in silence.

During the Holocaust 1935/45

If Jews don't look after themselves, we can be sure that no one else will.

In America there is one President for two hundred million people. In Israel, there is one President for three million presidents.

119

JUDGEMENT

Before I pass a judgement on a man, let me walk a mile in his moccasins.

Native American saying

The seat of knowledge is in the head; of wisdom, in the heart. We are sure to judge wrong if we do not feel that it is right.

Hazlitt

Judge not, that ye be not judged.

Matthew 7:1

We shall all of us have enough to do, without sitting in judgement upon other folks.

Walter Scott

Consider not only what a person has done but also consider why the person did it. Do not judge an action by external and/or so-called established standards but rather judge on the basis of the motives.

Don't judge a man by whether or not you like him personally; judge him by how well he performs. Judge a man by his foes as well as by his friends.

J. Conrad

All complain of want of memory but none of want of judgement.

Those directly involved are probably the least equipped to judge dispassionately the long-term results of their actions.

A good and faithful judge prefers what is right to what is expedient.

Horace

Try the manners of different nations firsthand before forming an opinion about them.

Robert Louis Stevenson

JUSTICE

Fairness and justice are not always identical.

It's about time that society started to show more compassion towards the victims instead of trying to find irrelevant excuses for the defendant's behaviour.

Most juries are right most of the time.

You go to court for law – not justice.

JUSTIFICATION

As usual, the important gave way to the urgent.

William Ronald Miller

You can justify almost any type of activity by calling it 'Research'.

MAS

You can justify almost any form of behaviour by saying that 'It is in the interests of safety.'

MAS

KINDNESS

Kindness consists of loving people more than they perhaps deserve.

Kindness is like cress seed; it increases by sowing.

Kindness is the language which the deaf can hear and the blind can read.

The kindly word that falls today may bear its fruit tomorrow.

A smile costs nothing but can achieve wonders.

Be grateful for every kindness.

No act of kindness, no matter how small, is ever wasted.

Aesop

Start a kind word on its travels; it may go far and do a lot of good.

KNOWLEDGE

The fat man knoweth not what the lean thinketh.

George Herbert

If a little knowledge is dangerous, where is the man who has so much as to be out of danger?

T.H. Huxley

It's not the things we don't know that cause us trouble. It's the things that we think we know but really don't know that do cause the trouble.

When a man's knowledge is not in order, the more of it he has the greater will be his confusion.

H. Spencer

Don't suppose; endeavour to know.

The man who knows most is the first to want to know more.

The afternoon knows what the morning never suspected.

The price one pays for pursuing any profession, or calling, is an intimate knowledge of its ugly side.

James Baldwin

It's better to know nothing than half-know a lot.

Friedrich Nietzsche

What the eye cannot see, the heart does not grieve over. Is knowledge, which may be alarming, better than unalarming ignorance?

W.F. Deedes

You may talk about anything, but do you know enough about it to be permitted more than two minutes on the subject?

Guessing is no substitute for knowledge.

MAS

LAUGHTER

He who laughs, lasts.

A day without a single laugh is a wasted day.

Nothing shows a man's character more than what he laughs at.

A laugh is a smile broken out of jail.

If you are going to be able to look back on something and laugh about it, you might as well laugh about it now.

M. Osmond

Take time to laugh. It is the music of the soul.

No matter how funny you think the joke is, if they don't laugh – take it out.

George Burns

You could be the meanest person in the world, but if you look long enough you will find something that brings a smile to your face.

Charles L. Shoup

LAW

Laws are like clothes; they must fit the people they are made for.

English laws punish vice; the Chinese laws do more, they reward virtue.

Elimination of corruption is not the number one priority of the Police Commissioner. His job is to enforce the law and to fight crime.

Matters of principle are the very last things that should provoke a man to seeking recourse in the law courts.

Len Deighton

Oh Lord, give us wise laws . . . and fewer of them.

LAWYERS

If there were no bad people there would be no good lawyers.

Stubborn men make lawyers rich.

A countryman between two lawyers is like a fish between two cats.

Benjamin Franklin

Talk is cheap, unless you happen to be talking to your lawyer.

Law is good for lawyers. They are the only people who can be sure of some success whenever a case comes to court. They always issue a fee account.

MAS

Old lawyers have long memories.

LAZINESS

The man who complains he is not getting enough is usually not giving enough.

Failure is more frequently from want of energy than from want of capital.

D. Webster

More people die of laziness than of hard work.

A lazy man is bad enough, but the man who wants to do it all is worse.

Nothing is easy to the unwilling.

He has this terrible trouble with his back. He has great difficulty in separating it from the mattress.

LEADERSHIP

Perhaps the most important responsibility of a director, and the most difficult to discharge, is provision of strategic leadership. What do we mean by 'strategy'? The forces definition is perhaps the most useful; to create the conditions in which an unwinnable battle may become winnable. It needs the ability to think ahead to a desired end-result and then work backwards to see what has to be done in what order to get there. This kind of thinking is obvious to anyone who has worked at the top of a company which knows where it is going. But it is rare to find this sort of thinking practised in government, and also too rare in business.

Strategic leadership requires one skill, if one can call it that. That is a readiness to risk looking personally foolish; a readiness to discuss half-baked ideas, because fully-baked ideas usually start out in that form; a total honesty, a readiness to admit that you have got it completely wrong. Above all, it needs the realisation that problems are solved and opportunities created by many minds working together, not by infallible autocrats.

The salutary influence of example.

A good leader takes a little more than his share of blame; a little less than his share of credit.

A.H. Glasgow

A strong leader knows that if he develops his associates he will be even stronger.

J.F. Lincoln

Good leadership implies consideration of those who follow. It requires a communication system that works both ways – from the bottom up, as well as from the top down.

Dr W. Menninger

Conductors of great symphony orchestras do not play every musical instrument; yet through leadership the ultimate production is an expressive and unified combination of tones.

T.D. Bailey

The very essence of leadership is that you have to have vision. You cannot blow an uncertain trumpet.

T. Hesburgh

'They're all following you.'
'No they're not. I just happen to be in front.'

Leadership is making people do things they would not normally do.

Claes Hultman

Leaders are like eagles; they don't flock and you find them one at a time.

Real leaders are ordinary people with extraordinary determination.

LEARNING

There was too much 'chalk and talk' and not sufficient 'hands on' training involved. People learn best by doing.

The elitism of learning and ability.

Learning without thinking is so much wasted energy.

Learning teaches you but one lesson: to doubt.

One is never too old to unlearn bad habits.

Cees Buddingh

Every time you learn something, you also have to learn when not to use it.

It is not hard to learn more. What is hard is to unlearn when you discover yourself wrong.

Martin H. Fischer

It's a lot easier to learn something if it's important to you.

Michael Dell

There is always much more to learn than there is to teach.

LIBERTY

We all declare for liberty, but in using the same word we do not all mean the same thing.

Abraham Lincoln

If we suffer tamely a lawless attack upon our liberty, we encourage it, and involve others in our doom.

Sam Adams

We must keep in the forefront of our minds the fact that whenever we take away the liberties of those whom we hate, we are opening the door to loss of liberty for those whom we love.

Wendell L. Willkie

LIES

A believable lie is not better than a stupid fact.

We lie loudest when we lie to ourselves.

It is seldom that any really good story is wholly true.

There are two kinds of lies. There are lies by distortion and lies by omission. Lies by omission are by far the most dangerous because there is nothing untrue in them, but what they do not tell you is often of critical importance.

MAS

Half a truth is often a great lie.

It's easy to lie when one is far away from home.

A liar needs to have a good memory.

When you say that you agree to a thing in principle, you may mean that you have not the slightest intention of carrying it out in practice.

Bismarck

Blessed are the forgetful; for they get the better even of their blunders.

Nietzsche

A lie revealed is still not necessarily the truth.

There are three kinds of lies: lies, damned lies and statistics.

Benjamin Disraeli

A lie can be halfway round the world before the truth has got its trousers on.

A little inaccuracy sometimes saves a ton of explanation.

H.H. Munro

LIFE

I live for the future, and not in or for the past.

It is almost a law of life that when one door closes on us, another opens. It only feels as though another one has slammed in our face.

It's an imperfect world, and we are all lifelong members.

Between the golden years of youth and the golden years of retirement come those nickel-plated years when you do all the work.

Bill Vaughan

What matters in life is not what you are but what you do.

The art of living is to live long and to die feeling young.

The optimist proclaims that we live in the best of all possible worlds; and the pessimist fears this is true.

James Branch Cabell

Man has made his bedlam; let him lie in it.

Fred Allen

Golden rule of life: never explain.

The proper function of man is to live, not to exist.

It matters not how a man dies, but how he lives.

Samuel Johnson

Life is six to four against.

Spike Milligan

Life is like riding a bicycle; you don't fall off unless you stop pedalling.

C. Pepper

If I had my life to live over, I would relax more. I wouldn't take so many things so seriously. I would take more chances. I would climb more mountains and swim more rivers . . . Next time I'd start barefooted earlier in the spring and stay that way later in the fall.

Frank Dickey

Make the most of your life. You are going to be a long time dead.

Life is what happens while you are making other plans.

Youth is a blunder; manhood a struggle; old age a regret.

Benjamin Disraeli

I love being alive. I have no wish to look at flowers from the wrong end.

This life is a test; it is only a test. If it were a real life, you would receive instructions on where to go and what to do.

There are no one-sided equations in life.

MAS

Life is a universally fatal sexually transmitted disease.

LIFE HEREAFTER

No matter how religious they are, they never want to leave this world in order to see the next world.

The spiritualist who died out of curiosity.

Everybody wants to go to heaven, but nobody wants to die.

If there is a life hereafter, I want to come back as a Yorkshire terrier in a Jewish household.

MAS

LIMITATIONS

The way for an executive to maintain good health is always to do one thing less than he thinks he can do.

Bernard M. Baruch

You cannot fly like an eagle with the wings of a wren.

Don't tell me what you can't do; tell me what you can do.

Sean Walsh

The college graduate is presented with a sheepskin to cover his commercial nakedness.

Non omnia possumus omnes – We can't all do everything.

Virgil

Do not let what you cannot do interfere with what you can do.

A bend in the road is not the end of the road . . . unless you fail to make the turn.

There are no barriers in life, only challenges.

LISTENING

Few people, broadly speaking, wish to hear what you have been doing.

Some people have little to say, but you have to listen a long time to find out.

Listen to others, but make up your own mind.

If you do not get the listener's attention in the first sentence, the remainder of your message is lost.

LOGIC

Small son to father: 'Why should lemonade spoil my dinner and martinis give you an appetite?'

F. Benson

A quick response is worth a thousand logical responses.

Merle P. Martin

Being logical does not always mean being right.

He had the kind of analytical mind that always sought logical answers to all situations.

LOOKING

If your look doesn't convince, your words won't either.

Grillparzer

Many people say that they did not see, when in fact they weren't even looking.

LOSING

Nice guys finish last.

Arnold Palmer

Second place is a niche in oblivion.

Jack Nicklaus

It is of little consequence to play well if you lose.

To lose and learn hurts no one: but to lose and NOT to learn – that is lasting tragedy.

Phyliss Bottome

He was a very bad loser in spite of having had so much practice at it.

Some performance, people! We have managed to snatch defeat from the jaws of victory.

Cyril Card

Show me a good loser and I'll show you a regular loser.

Winning may not be everything, but losing isn't anything.

You are not beaten until you admit it.

There are no prizes for good losers.

Victory has a hundred fathers. Defeat is an orphan.

Losers always whine about having done their best.

He who fears being conquered is sure of defeat.

Napoleon

When you lose, don't lose the lesson.

LOVE

Love is the triumph of imagination over intelligence.

H.L. Mencken

Flirting is the gentle art of making a man feel pleased with himself.

Helen Rowland

The only difference in the game of love over the last few thousand years is that they've changed trumps from clubs to diamonds.

Love has the power of making you believe what you would normally treat with the greatest suspicion.

As Mark Antony said to Cleopatra 'Non sum hinc ut dicerem' which roughly translated says 'I'm not here to talk.'

It wasn't love at first sight. The first time I met him I didn't know he was rich.

The difference between true love and herpes is that herpes lasts for ever.

Jim Baumgarten

Real love begins where nothing is expected in return.
Antoine de Saint-Exupéry

Love is not looking into each other's eyes, but looking together in the same direction.
Antoine de Saint-Exupéry

LOVERS

All the world loves a lover, unless he is in a telephone kiosk.

A great lover is not a man who romances a different woman every night. A great lover is a man who romances the same woman every night.

If all the world loves a lover, why are there hotel detectives?

LUCK

I find the harder I practice, the luckier I am.
Gary Player

Luck helps most when you don't rely upon it too much.

Of course I believe in luck. How otherwise can you explain the success of the people you detest?
Jean Cocteau

Only with the help of luck can you expect to see something without specifically looking for it.

'What rotten, lousy luck . . . '
'Is there any other kind?'

Luck is something a man goes to some lengths to create.

Robin Moore

Luck is the idol of the idle.

Better to be lucky than clever.

Jim Brown

I have always maintained that whether a black cat crossing your path is lucky or unlucky depends on whether you are a man or a mouse.

Bernard Levin

MAKE-UP OF MANKIND

The meeting of two personalities is like the contact of two chemical substances: if there is any reaction, both are transformed.

Carl Gustav Jung

Omit a few of the abstruse sciences, and mankind's study of man occupies nearly the whole field of literature. The burden of history is what man has been; of law, what he does; of physiology, what he is; of ethics, what he ought to be; of revelation, what he shall be.

G. Finlayson

I came to the Greeks early and found answers in them – Greeks thought each human being different and I take a lot of comfort in the fact that my fingerprints are different from anybody else's.

Edith Hamilton

Earnest people are often people who habitually look on the serious side of things that have no serious side.

Van Wyck Brooks

Nature has made two sorts of excellent intellects; one kind to produce beautiful thoughts or actions, the other to admire them.

Joseph Joubert

Another thing that makes man unique is that he is the only living thing that needs advice on how to grow old.

J.M. Loughlin

No excellent soul is exempt from a mixture of madness.

Aristotle

All really serious people give an impression of serenity.

Alain Resnais

The world's great men have not commonly been great scholars, nor its great scholars great men.

Oliver Wendell Holmes

The trouble with the world is that the stupid are cocksure and the intelligent are full of doubt.

Man never made any material as resilient as the human spirit.

Bern Williams

We all have our little monsters. The trick is to recognise them. When you've done that, living with them is easy.

Campbell Armstrong

Some people make things happen, some watch things happen, while the others wonder what has happened.

Excellence is the best deterrent to racialism and sexism.

Rev. Jesse Jackson

Sex: The expense is damnable, the pleasure momentary and the position ludicrous.

Lord Chesterfield

MANAGEMENT

Planning and control are synonymous with good management.

In terms of human resources, which are after all the key to a nation's future, we are an underdeveloped country. From top to bottom, we are underskilled. Many of our younger people lack even the basic education needed to take part in the economic process. We are short of people with technical skills. Senior managers and company directors are notoriously weak in the understanding of financial management.

No man will ever be a big executive who feels that he must, either openly or under cover, follow up every order he gives and see that it is done; nor will he ever develop a capable assistant.

John Mahin

'Regulate the behaviour of people' to accomplish a project.

Executives are paid to make strength productive.

139

Situations which are barely manageable today may become unmanageable tomorrow.

The best executive is the one who has sense enough to pick good men to do what he wants done, and self-restraint enough to keep from meddling with them while they do it.

Theodore Roosevelt

Never tell people how to do things. Tell them what to do and they will surprise you with their ingenuity.

General George S. Patton

Management can best show it cares by doing what works; by getting results.

Price Pritchett, Ron Pound

MARRIAGE

Keep your eyes wide open before marriage; half shut afterwards.

It is not lack of love but lack of friendship that makes unhappy marriages.

F. Nietzsche

Advice for new brides:- Never refuse him anything he asks. Observe a certain amount of reserve and delicacy before him. Keep up the honeymoon romance whether at home or in the desert. At the same time do not make prudish bothers, which only disgust and are not true modesty. Never permit anyone to speak disrespectfully of him before you, and if anyone does, no matter how difficult, leave the room. Never permit anyone to tell you anything about him, especially of his conduct with regard to other women. Always keep his heart up when he has made a failure.

Isabel Arundel

Marriage is a mutual admiration society where one person is always in the right and the other one is the husband.

W. Grant

Marriage is an alliance between a man who cannot sleep with the window open and a woman who cannot sleep with the window shut.

'How is your wife/husband?'
'Compared to whom?'

Marriage is a process by which a man finds out the sort of husband his wife thinks she should have had.

Many a man who marries a wisp of a girl is astonished at the will o' the wisp.

T. April

Mother to distraught young bride. 'There are three things that you cannot do: you cannot keep a floor clean, you cannot keep a baby dry and you cannot stop a man from wandering.'

Some men feel that the only thing they owe the woman who marries them is a grudge.

Helen Rowland

The honeymoon is not actually over until we cease to stifle our sighs and begin to stifle our yawns.

Helen Rowland

Do not marry for money – marry where money is.

Many a man in love with a dimple makes the mistake of marrying the whole girl.

First Law of Marriage: Presents equal guilt.

Holy acrimony is another name for marriage.

Father does not hear what Mother says, but Mother hears what Father does not say.

The advantage of being married to an archaeologist is that the older you get, the more interested he becomes in you.
Agatha Christie

MATHEMATICS

Just as the fancy of the little boy is led on by the chalk in his hand, so physicists are leaning on mathematics which constantly reveals beauties and harmonies beyond our imagination.
Niels Bohr

Mathematics deals exclusively with the relations of concepts to each other without consideration of their relation to experience.
Albert Einstein

How can you do 'New Math' problems with an 'Old Math' mind?
Charles Schulz

The mathematician is a kind of Frenchman. You tell him something; he translates it into his own language; and at once it is something else.

Goethe

You have to count pretty high before you find a number containing the letter 'A'. The answer, though hard to believe, is one thousand.

Davenport

At the present time our only way of understanding the ultimate character of the physical world is through mathematical reasoning. We don't know any other way of describing it accurately or seeing the interrelationships. So I don't think a person who hasn't developed some mathematical sense is capable of fully appreciating this aspect of the world.

Richard Feynman

MATURITY

The older I grow, the more I distrust the familiar doctrine that age brings wisdom.

H.L. Mencken

Admitting we are wrong is a modest way of showing we have grown wiser.

Jonathan Swift

A boy becomes an adult about three years before his parents think he does – and about five years after he thinks he does.

To judge maturity by the criterion of age is an immature thought in itself.

William J. Abercrombie

You're only young once, but some people can be immature for ever.

The yearning to attribute legal blame for all manner of human misfortunes is a symptom of immaturity.

The first sign of maturity is the discovery that the volume control also turns to the left.

How old you are is not as important as how you are old.

With maturity comes an ability to assess the past with objective eyes.

Eric Lustbader

MAXIMS

All good maxims are available to everybody: they only need to be applied.

MEDICINE

Only the man who believes in it can be cured by the medicine he takes.

Saying 'Gesundheit' doesn't really help the common cold – but it's about as good as anything the doctors have come up with.

All our slogans and all our health campaigns will not heal one sick person.

MEMORY

Memory is the perfume of the soul.

George Sand

Harsh lessons make for long memories.

Remembrances embellish life whilst forgetfulness only makes it endurable.

I'll never forget eh, what's his name?

J. Leslie Wolfson

A memory is an etching that time has engraved upon your mind.

Richard Brown

Whenever your memory starts to let you down, and you can't remember the details of a particular event, it might be said that you were experiencing a 'senior moment'.

MEN

A good wife and health are a man's greatest riches.

No man can sink so low that a woman or a dog won't love him.

Men fall into three classes – the handsome, the intelligent and the majority.

Men have a much better time of it than women; for one thing, they marry later and for another thing, they die earlier.

H.L. Mencken

Men have as exaggerated an idea of their rights as women have of their wrongs.

E.W. Howe

Man is a polygamous creature.

MAS

Men still find it very difficult to cope with successful women.

He was a good man as good men go, and as good men go, he went.

Blues song

There has been only one indispensable man – Adam.

There are three things real men cannot say:
'I'm wrong.'
'I'm lost.'
'I can't fix it.'

MENDING

You can't get two men to mend a watch.

You can't fix it if you don't know what is broken.

If it ain't broke, don't fix it.

MINDS

Private property began the instant somebody had a mind of his own.

E.E. Cummings

The true standard of quality is seated in the mind; those who think nobly are noble.

I. Bickerstaffe

Depression is a disorder of feelings, of emotions. It is not a disorder of the mind.

Great minds do great things in a simple manner.

The mind grows rich from what it receives, the heart from what it gives.

I agree with no man's opinion. I have a mind of my own.

Ivan Turgenev

A mind once stretched by a new idea, never regains its original dimensions.

MINUTIAE

If at first you don't succeed, read the instructions.

Read the small print. It seems curious that the critical conditions and clauses are hidden amongst less important material and are printed in the smallest size of type used in the document. If the content is of consequence it should be given prominence, and not tucked away so that it is not likely to be found and its significance recognised. Until such time when legal morality applies, read the small print.

MAS

MISFORTUNE

If all our misfortunes were laid in one common heap, whence everyone must take an equal portion, most people would be happy to take their own and depart.

Socrates

MISTAKES

A man who has committed a mistake and doesn't correct it is committing another mistake.

Confucius

Learning from your mistakes is an expensive way of getting ahead.

To get maximum attention, it's hard to beat a good, big mistake.

He who sees his own mistakes has no time to consider those of others.

It's not hard to admit errors that are only cosmetically wrong.

J.K. Galbraith

It's better to trip over with your feet than with your tongue.

We all have fears of making mistakes, saying the wrong thing or looking foolish. Some show it less than others but it is always there. Don't let these fears restrict your thinking or expression. It is certain that every good idea or new process is surrounded by the debris of ideas and solutions that were voiced and rejected. Unfortunately, the light of success, with the schemes that do work, overshadows this debris and we forget it exists. Don't be afraid to speak up. Few great solutions are flashes of inspiration. They are simply the top of the pyramid, supported by a substructure of rejected ideas.

MAS

The world is littered with the results of wrong decisions. If Brunel's broad gauge railway had become standard, the railways might still be able to compete against road transport. The VHS videotape, now ubiquitous, eliminated the superior Betamax format. The pressurised water reactor is the dominant nuclear power source but it is neither the safest nor most efficient. The situation we are faced with today is only the latest in a long, miserable tradition of make-do-and-mend systems, cobbled up to try to compensate for past mistakes.

Chris Partridge, Roger Highfield

The only man who never makes a mistake is the man who never does anything.

Theodore Roosevelt

Everyone is wrong, except the wrong-doer.

You can make any number of mistakes in life, provided they are not big ones.

The greatest mistake a man can make is to be afraid of making one.

MONEY

Whether you're rich or poor, it's nice to have money.

Joe Kingsley

Money is not everything. A man with nine million pounds can be just as happy as the man with ten million.

Among the things that money can't buy is what it used to.

W. Short

All this wheeling and dealing around, why, it isn't for money, it's for fun. Money's just the way we keep score.

Henry Tyroon

Our relative poverty will only be overcome when we become more interested in the creation of wealth rather than its distribution and consumption.

Brain Drain Committee Report 1967

Money may not buy happiness, but with it you can be unhappy in comfort.

Is there any such thing as a safe investment? Is there any investment that is not a speculation?

Max Gunther

Money does not change men. It merely unmasks them.

Petronella Wyatt

Money speaks all tongues.

Wooden dollars represent unreal money – like depreciation and reserves. No one can spend them.

Money isn't everything, but it certainly keeps the children in touch.

Money can't buy friends, but it gets you a better class of enemy.

Whoever says money can't buy happiness doesn't know where to shop.

Give, never lend. If a friend tries to borrow money, first ask him why he does not go to a banker. No one likes a lender.

Money is a commodity, a business tool.

Stuart Sim

Money has always interested me as a measurement of human activities. It is a scorekeeper.

Claes Hultman

'What is the most powerful force on earth?'
'Compound interest.'

Albert Einstein

Money doesn't buy happiness, it only buys more happiness.

Louis Phillips

When it comes to stock markets, I'd rather be a lucky fool than an unlucky genius.

David Walton

MONITORING

Has anybody bothered to monitor the results?

Donald Trelford

That which has been obtained by so much effort can only be retained by so much vigilance.

Marjorie Phillips

Who will watch the watchers?

Juvenal

MOTHERS

A mother is not a person to lean on but a person to make leaning unnecessary.

D.C. Fisher

When you educate a man you educate an individual; when you educate a woman you educate a whole family.

C.D. McIver

One of the world's mysteries is where mothers learn all the things they tell their daughters not to do.

Many mothers will do anything for their children – except let them be themselves.

MOTIVATION

We are all ready to be savage in some cause. The difference between a good man and a bad one is the choice of the cause.

W. James

Everybody is motivated by thought of reward or fear of punishment.

A farmer berated his dog for being unable to catch a chicken. 'Correct' said the dog, 'but there is a subtle difference in motivation. I was running for my dinner – he was running for his life.'

MAS

Are you playing to win, or are you only taking part in the game?

The truly great man does not strive to obtain honours.
He does strive to deserve them.

Confucius

The difference between an ordinary person and a successful person is not a lack of strength, not a lack of knowledge, but rather a lack of will.

MOTORING

It's the overtakers that keep the undertakers busy.

A woman asked her husband, 'Be an angel and let me drive.' He did, and he is.

Bob Goddard

I remember my first ride in a Rolls-Royce, a chariot drawn by winged horses.

There are too many motorists who treat traffic lights as a suggestion and not as an instruction.

MAS

MUSIC

Music is the only language in which you cannot say a mean or sarcastic thing.

J. Erskine

Music is a language devoid of bitterness.

If you have to ask what jazz is, you'll never know.

Louis Armstrong

La Bohème is a most enjoyable opera. It also benefits from being the shortest.

Dancing is just walking to music.

Bernard Silver

NECESSITY

Necessity is the plea for every infringement of human freedom. It is the argument of tyrants; it is the creed of slaves.

William Pitt

Necessity is the mother of taking chances.

Mark Twain

NEGATIVITY

It is the greatest of all mistakes to do nothing because you fear you can only do a little. Do what you can.

Sidney Smith

If you have the capability to be a great musician, don't sit around and whine that you never will be a great painter.

Kim Woo-Choong

If you spend your whole life waiting for the storm you'll never enjoy the sunshine.

Morris West

We are not retreating – we are advancing in another direction.

General Douglas MacArthur

NOSTALGIA

Nostalgia is not what it used to be.

The older you get the more practical, even cynical, you get, and you may tend to lose sight of the beauty in life. Nostalgia, memories, filter out a lot of the bad things that happen to you, the things that hide the beauty, and let you live an idealised past.

William Ronald Miller

NOVELTY

Novelty is short lived. After four days all respect for it is gone.

There are three things which the public will always clamour for, namely: Novelty, Novelty and Novelty.

Thomas Hood

OBEDIENCE

I just wish that people would do what they are told. If they think that something could be improved then please let them say so. But that's all. Every time someone thinks or uses their initiative, it costs me money.

Dan Carlaw

We can avoid a lot of work if we will simply play by the new rules.

Price Pritchett, Ron Pound

OBJECTIONS

Nothing will ever be attempted if all objections must first be overcome.

Samuel Johnson

OBJECTIVES

There is no sense in hitting bull's eyes on the wrong targets.

If you don't know what you really want, you're likely to go astray.

You will never get anywhere if you don't know where you're going.

You can't score goals if you haven't got any goalposts.

Objectives must be realistic: but they must also be challenging in order to create a sense of urgency in the Company.

I believe in picking simple targets.
Then you allow people to achieve them.

David A. G. Simon

It is most unlikely that anyone will ever fulfil their every wish and ambition so, probably, we will all leave this world with heartfelt cries of 'If only'. A practicable objective in life should be to try to make the size of the 'If only' pile as small as possible.

MAS

MEMORANDUM

The objective of all dedicated employees should be to thoroughly analyse all situations, anticipate all problems prior to their occurrence, have answers for all these problems and move swiftly to solve these problems when called upon.

However . . .

when you are up to your ass in alligators, it can be difficult to remind yourself that your initial objective was to drain the swamp.

It is essential for people to have dragons. The clever thing is to pick dragons small enough that they present a meaningful challenge that you can handle, but not so big that they will devour you.

For the target that you have in mind, is it more appropriate to use a shotgun or a sniper's rifle?

MAS

Set personal goals. Give yourself a sense of purpose.

Price Pritchett, Ron Pound

Women dally in sex, looking for love.
Men dally in love, looking for sex.

OBLIGATIONS

A promise made is a debt unpaid.

Robert Service

Don't ask favours, and you won't owe any.

One gambles to win, but one must pay one's debts if one loses.

Confucius

OBSESSION

There is only a thin line between inspiration and obsession.

Dedication is one thing, obsession is something else entirely.

There's nobody more dangerous than a sincere visionary.
Morris West

OBSTINACY

He can never be good that is not obstinate.

Beliefs and convictions: all locked away from the light of reason.

An obstinate man is ruled by a fool.

Can't and won't!
Sally Wassell

An obstinate man doesn't have opinions – they have him.
Alexander Pope

A fanatic is one who can't change his mind and won't change the subject.
Winston S. Churchill

OPINION

If all mankind minus one were of one opinion, and only one person were of the contrary opinion, mankind would be no more justified in silencing that one person than he, if he had the power, would be justified in silencing mankind. We can never be sure that the opinion we are trying to stifle is false opinion and even if we were sure, stifling it would still be evil.

John Stuart Mill

Opinions cannot survive if one has no chance to fight for them.

T. Mann

The dissenting opinions of one generation become the prevailing philosophy of the next.

Hendrick

The difficult part of an argument is not to defend one's opinion, but rather to know it.

A. Maurois

An opinion loses none of its validity just because you don't act according to it.

Faced with the choice between changing one's mind and proving there is no need to do so, almost everyone gets busy on the proof.

Every new opinion, at its starting, is precisely a minority one.

Opinion is ultimately determined by the feelings, and not by the intellect.

Herbert Spencer

If you are going to drain the pond, don't ask the frogs for their opinion.

There is no right or wrong; there is only opinion.

OPPORTUNITY

Seize the day – I'm sure that there were people on the *Titanic* who refused a dessert.

But the system doesn't promise equal status; it promises equal opportunities.

Starve the problems: feed the opportunities.

Don't minimise risk: maximise opportunity.

Four things come not back: the spoken word, the sped arrow, time past and the neglected opportunity.

The reason a lot of people do not recognise an opportunity when they meet it is that it usually goes around looking like hard work.

There is but one time to do a thing and that is the first.
General George S. Patton

Life is short, the future uncertain; therefore don't waste opportunities.

If you are a person who lives alone, don't say 'No, thank you' to invitations. If you say 'No' this time, you may not get the chance to say 'Yes, please' another time.

You don't get a second chance to make a first impression.

A pessimist sees the difficulty in every opportunity; an optimist sees the opportunity in every difficulty.
Winston S. Churchill

OPTIMISM

Cast your bread on the waters; it may not all come back soggy.

MAS

Too many people live in the belief that someone will take care of the distant tomorrow. Who is this mysterious someone, and what will they do, and with what resources?

Give me your hand, and we'll cross over the bridge. Give me your heart and we will fly over the moon.

Tina Coetzee

OVER-REACTION

Never call in a tiger to chase away a dog.

Don't put up your umbrella before it has started to rain.

Never cut through a knot you can undo with your fingers.

Blowing up a bear with dynamite brings no meat to the hunter.

Chinese saying

PAIN

A bee's sting is only one-thirty-second of an inch long. The other five inches is imagination.

D. Marshall

Learn to smile – even if it pains you.

The ache in my heart is a black sea of pain.

Eric Bogle

If you want to feel guilty, call your mother.

A sharp pain, like ice cream biting into your teeth.

Pain is temporary; glory is forever.

PARENTS

If parents would only realise how they bore their children.

George Bernard Shaw

Having children makes you no more a parent than having a piano makes you a pianist.

Michael Levine

Parentage is a very important profession; but no test for fitness for it is ever imposed.

George Bernard Shaw

PATIENCE

Everything ends well for the one who has patience.

Tolstoy

Patience achieves more than strength and fury.

La Fontaine

The greatest power is often simple patience. Lord, give me patience, but hurry.

PAYMENT

Pay as you go. If you cannot pay – don't go.

The three most beautiful words in the English language are 'Find cheque enclosed.'

Dorothy Parker

PEACE

Since wars begin in the minds of men, it is in the minds of men that the defence of peace must be constructed.

Clement Attlee

Peace is indivisible.

Peace cannot be kept by force; it can only be achieved by understanding.

Albert Einstein

Fame and tranquillity can never be bedfellows.

Montaigne

If everyone looked on his neighbour as a friend then there would be no need for war, and peace would ensue.

PERFECTION

If all the world were just, there would be no need of valour.

Plutarch

During a period of exciting discovery or progress there is no time to plan the perfect headquarters. The time for that comes later, when all the important work has been done. Perfection, we know, is finality; and finality is death.

C. Northcote Parkinson

Strive for perfection in everything you do.

Henry Royce

Aim at perfection in everything, though in most cases it is unattainable. However, they who aim at it, and persevere, will come much nearer to it than those whose laziness and despondency make them give it up as unattainable.

Lord Chesterton

There are no perfect men – only perfect intentions.

There was this man who spent his life looking for the ideal woman; and he found her. Unfortunately, she was looking for the ideal man.

It is not possible to claim that a system or plan is perfect or error-free. The best that can be said is that, so far, the system has not failed any of the tests to which it has been subjected.

MAS

Perfection is achieved, not only when there is nothing left to add, but when there is nothing left to take away.

Antoine de Saint-Exupéry

PERMANENCE

I have learned to accept a thing once done as done; we must take the consequences, and there's no sense in debating it as though it were still to do.

It is wise to keep in mind that no success or failure is necessarily permanent.

PERSEVERANCE

Consider the postage stamp: it sticks to one thing until it gets there.

If you have a good idea, never be downhearted if you meet with early reverses. As in most things in life, it is stubborn perseverance that wins in the end.

David Moreau

'Having what it takes' is not just a measure of ability. It shows also application, determination to succeed and persistence. Only possession of all these qualities qualifies a person as 'having what it takes'.

By trying, we can easily learn to endure adversity. Another man's, I mean.

Mark Twain

My task was to give the best in me. I am content that I did so, but to lose is to be reminded forcefully of some essentials: that sometimes our best isn't good enough; that we can't solve every problem or win every battle; and that sometimes life is terribly unfair. But if we want to keep living with ourselves, we must keep on trying.

Perseverance performs greater works than strength.

People will persist in old ways unless you make it impossible for them to do so.

MAS

Perseverance is not a long race; it is many short races one after another.

Walter Elliott

Smart is good, but thorough is better. Give me thorough over smart every time.

Campbell Armstrong

We are built on dreams, perseverance and commitment to excellence.

Persistence prevails when all else fails.

PERSUASION

A man persuaded against his will, remaineth unpersuaded still.

You can get more with a kind word and a gun than you can with a kind word alone.

Al Capone

PHILOSOPHY

Your view of the valley is conditioned by the hill upon which you choose to stand.

MAS

The things a man believes most profoundly are rarely on the surface of his mind or on the tip of his tongue. Newly acquired notions, formulas learned by rote from books, decisions based upon expediency, the fashionable ideas of the moment – these are right at the top of the pile, ready to be sampled and displayed in bright after-dinner conversation. But the ideas that make up a man's philosophy of life are somewhere way down below.

Eric Johnson

He who knows, and knows he knows, he is a wise man – seek him.
He who knows, and knows not he knows, he is asleep – wake him.
He who knows not, and knows he knows not, he is a child – teach him.
But he who knows not, and knows not he knows not, he is a fool – shun him.

Good food and philosophy don't mix.

Morris West

PITY

It is better to arouse other people's envy than their pity.

PLANS

A man who does not think and plan long ahead will find trouble right at his door.

Confucius

The trail of business progress is littered with the debris of outworn management devices . . . Plans, systems and concepts have a rate of obsolescence just as does a piece of machinery . . . Originally serving appropriate purposes, they tend to become encrusted with habit and tradition to a point where they actually become deterrents to fresh thinking.

M.P. McNair

'I have a plan.'
'So had General Custer.'

A plan that can't be altered is a bad plan anyway.

Systematic thinking must precede action.

As well as certain gifts of mind, a planner must have gifts of character. He must be intellectually honest; all the facts must be surveyed, not a selection congenial to himself or his employer. He must be morally honest. He must say to himself 'I am not concerned with policy in the political sense. I am only concerned with analysing the situation and with the inferences that follow.' Moreover, he is going to have to say 'I shall eventually come up with a specific recommendation, or a set of specific recommendations, but not with alternatives or compromises for each member of the set.'

The critical six Ps of industry, commerce and general life: Pre Planning Prevents Piss Poor Performance.

Lack of planning on your part does not constitute an emergency on my part.

My plans are still in embryo. In case you've never been there, this is a small town on the outskirts of wishful thinking.

Groucho Marx

PLEASURE

'Why would a man do such a thing?' The more pertinent
question would be 'If any man finds such joy in a given act, why
would he do anything else?'

It is not often that I combine business with pleasure – but you're
fired!

You can't please anyone else, if what you do doesn't please you
too.

The reward of a thing well done, is to have done it.

Ralph Waldo Emerson

Don't complain that the rose bush has thorns; rejoice that the
thornbush bears roses.

Koran

Take time to play. It is the secret of perpetual youth.

Illusion is the first of all pleasures.

Voltaire

It is not doing the things we like to do, but liking the things we
have to do that makes life pleasant.

POEMS

I think that I shall never see
A billboard lovely as a tree.
Indeed, unless the billboards fall
I'll never see a tree at all.

Ogden Nash

I sneezed a sneeze into the air,
It fell to earth, I know not where.
But hard and froze were the looks of those
In whose vicinity I snooze.

POLICY

Cost is a fact; price is a policy.

Maximum speed is a fact; driving speed is a policy.

POLITENESS

A man gracious and courteous to strangers is truly a citizen of the world.

Politeness is to human nature what warmth is to wax.
A. Schopenhauer

Politeness costs you nothing. Impoliteness can cost you dear.

Dignity and courtesy should prevail, always.

Never insult the absent.

All doors open to courtesy.
Thomas Fuller

Politeness is goodwill in small things.
Macaulay

Politeness is the lubricant of civilized society.

POLITICS

In a country well governed, poverty is something to be ashamed of. In a country badly governed, wealth is something to be ashamed of.

Confucius

In political discussion, heat is in inverse proportion to knowledge.

Statesmen face facts; politicians distort them.

I am not a politician, and my other habits are also good.

A. Ware

Politics are almost as exciting as war, and quite as dangerous. In war, you can only be killed once . . .

Winston S. Churchill

The trouble with politicians and dictators is that they speak a load of bullshit and the great mass, like cattle lining up at the trough, devour it wholesale.

Campbell Armstrong

A police state is a country run by criminals.

Robert Harris

Never forget: one man's right is another man's wrong.

Ninety per cent of politics is deciding who to blame.

Meg Greenfield

One man's freedom fighter is another man's terrorist.

His views were to the right of Attila the Hun.

Politics is war without bloodshed, while war is politics with bloodshed.

Mao Tse-Tung

Political systems are as imperfect and corrupt as the men who design them.

Morris West

Instead of giving a politician the keys of the city, it might be better to change the locks.

Doug Larson

The language of politics is contrived for the concealment of truth.

Morris West

A politician thinks of the next election.
A statesman thinks of the next generation.

POPULARITY

To be popular yourself you must first learn to like other people. There is just no other way.

One way for a youngster to be popular is to be able to play the piano. Another way is to have a rich father.

Popularity is not always a good gauge of a man's worth.

Richard M. Nixon

POSITIVITY

If one may be presumptuous enough to offer advice to computer users:
    Decide the objective;
    Define the problems;
    Choose the solution;
    Keep it simple and stop for nothing.
Equally this is probably a sound method for tackling any project.

Don't curse the dark – light a candle.

Never look back. Try harder in future.

It is never too late to be what you might have been.

George Eliot

People can be classified, broadly, into fighters and the self-indulgent. If you want to have a chance of winning, the approach is straightforward. Don't whine. Don't ask for charity. Don't go under with booze. You must be willing to fight for what you feel strongly about.

Man lives in the here and now, not in the perhaps.

Morris West

The opera's never over till the fat lady sings.

W.T. Tyler

Rome did not create a great empire by having meetings; they did it by killing all those who opposed them.

POSSESSION

We believe in wider ownership – houses, shares, pension schemes, savings – property in all its forms. For ownership brings dignity, self-respect, independence and security for the future. It is a fundamental freedom.

I would rather sit on a pumpkin, and have it all to myself, than to be crowded on a velvet cushion.

Thoreau

We only possess the things we put to use.

La Fontaine

Many don't know what to do with their wealth but simply possess it.

Otto Weiss

Be not anxious about what you have, but about what you are.

Pope St Gregory I

Knowledge is the one possession no one can rob you of.

What difference does it make how much you have?
What you do not have amounts to much more.

Seneca

Beware of the mania for owning things.

It's not what you have, but who you know, that matters.

A gentleman does not make specific references to another man's possessions.

The more you own the more you are possessed.
Keep free of material things and enjoy life as it comes.
Marjorie Phillips

You can't have everything. Where would you put it?
Stephen Wright

POVERTY

He'll soon be a beggar that cannot say 'No.'

Poverty is no disgrace but there is little else to be said for it.

Poverty is a state of mind induced by a neighbour's new car.

What on earth will today's younger generation be able to tell their children they had to do without?
O. Arnold

You cannot help the poor by destroying the rich.

The worst kind of shame is being ashamed of frugality or poverty.

No one is so poor as the man who is unable to give anything away.

'Please help me, sir. I am really very poor and have nothing in the world except this little gun . . .'

Nobody should be allowed to die because they cannot afford to live.

Poverty is owning a horse.

When I give food to the poor, they call me a saint.
When I ask why the poor have no food, they call me a communist.

Dom Helder Camara

POWER

When you've got them by the balls, their hearts and minds will soon follow.

Richard M. Nixon

In this world there are the righteous and unrighteous. It is the righteous who decide who are the unrighteous.

Real power doesn't strike hard but it hits the target.

There is a difference between authorisation and power. Authorisation will allow you discretion, either limited or wide. Power gives you complete control of your actions.

Take time to think. It is the source of power.

Power is not something you get; it is something you grab.

Claes Hultman

Corporate bodies are more corrupt and profligate than individuals because they have more power to do mischief and are less amenable to disgrace or punishment. They feel neither shame, remorse, gratitude nor goodwill.

William Hazlitt

Any man can stand adversity; if you want to test a man's character, give him power.

Abraham Lincoln

In the land of the blind, the one-eyed man is king.

Power implies that we can accomplish what we plan.
Authority signifies only that we may order it to be accomplished.

Morris West

Never underestimate the power of very stupid people in large groups.

PRAISE

Baloney is flattery so thick that it cannot be true, and blarney is flattery so thin we like it.

F.J. Sheen

Don't ask for criticism if all you are after is praise.

Praise does wonders for the sense of hearing.

I can live for two months on a good compliment.

Mark Twain

PRAYER

The man who wants to learn to pray should go to sea.

The wish to pray is a prayer in itself.

Bernanos

Keep them productive, Lord, and lead them not into laziness, but deliver them from booze and dames and such.

Harold Ross

Oh Lord, help me keep my big mouth shut until I know what I'm talking about.

God grant me the serenity to accept the things I cannot change; the courage to change the things I can change and the wisdom to know the difference.

Lord, grant that we may always be right for thou knowest we will never change our minds.
Rev. Dr Houston

Teach us, Lord, to meet adversity; but not before it arrives.
The Talmud

Lord, give me the strength to land one so big that when telling of it later, I will have no cause to lie.

Dear God, please don't let me f_ _k up.
Alan B. Shepard (Mercury astronaut)

Please God, let me prove that winning the lottery won't spoil me.

PREFERENCE

I'd rather have him in the tent, pissing out, than outside the tent, pissing in.
Lyndon B. Johnson

PREJUDICE

A man is not good or bad for his actions. Good or bad is an assessment by other people, based upon their own prejudices.

To be prejudiced is always to be weak.

S. Johnson

Don't mistake your prejudices for principles.

A prejudiced person is one who doesn't believe in the same things as we do.

A great many people believe they are thinking when they are merely re-arranging their prejudices.

Prejudice (as a noun): A vagrant opinion without visible means of support.

Ambrose Bierce

The difference between a conviction and a prejudice is that you can explain a conviction without getting angry.

PRETENCE

Omne ignotum pro magnifico; anything little known is assumed to be wonderful.

Don't deny what you want for the sake of appearances.

The brave music of a distant drum.

You can pretend to be serious; you can't pretend to be witty.

Sacha Guitry

PROBLEMS

A problem well stated is a problem half solved.

C.F. Kettering

It isn't that they can't see the solution.
It is that they can't see the problem.

G.K. Chesterton

He has painted himself into a corner and now he is waiting for the paint to dry.

Drowning problems in an ocean of information is not the same as solving them.

When I am working on a problem, I never think about beauty. I think only of how to solve the problem. But when I have finished, if the solution is not beautiful I know it is wrong.

W. Buckminster Fuller

Obstacles are things a person sees when he takes his eyes off his goal.

Don't let what you are unable to do get in the way of what you are able to do.

Don't see problems; see challenges and opportunities.

Sometimes you must try to do the thing that you neither wish to do, nor believe that you are capable to do.

Today's problems are tomorrow's memories.

Marjorie Phillips

If you have no problems then you have no business.

Paul Jackson

PROFIT

What we want are profit centres; NOT cost centres.

Profit is a must. There can be no security for any employee in any business that doesn't make money. There can be no growth for that business. There can be no opportunities for the individual to achieve his personal ambitions unless his Company makes money.

D.C. Menzies

We are born with nothing. All that happens afterwards is clear profit.

We're not quite in the red – but I'm afraid we've reached a blush-pink stage.

The worst failure of a captain of industry is to fail to show a profit.

Samuel Gompers

In a free market, profit is society's reward for those who serve its interests.

Kazuo Inamori

There is a world of difference between 'profit' and 'profitability'.

MAS

The success of a business is measured by its profitability; not by its profit.

MAS

PROGRAMS

If you have any type of involvement with computers, or
computing systems, be wholly unsympathetic towards 'bugs'.
This is only a buzz word for mistakes and giving them a fancy
title should not lessen the responsibility of those who made the
mistakes. Technical failures may be attributable to mechanical
failure but human errors should be recognised as such. After all,
how patient and sympathetic would you be with your plumber if
your bath kept overflowing and he explained this by saying, 'It's
nothing. It's just a bug in the drainage system.'

MAS

A program will do what you tell it to do, not what you want it to
do.

Don't debug programs; debug the logic of the program beforehand.

Why is it that there is always time to correct errors in the
programs, but never enough time to do the job right the first
time round?

In every non-trivial program there is at least one bug.

One man's constant is another man's variable.

If you don't know what your program is supposed to do, you'd
better not start writing it.

Dijkstra

There used to be a software magazine with the title of 'Oh, By
The Way'. Somebody was very perceptive.

PROGRESS

True education makes for inequality: the inequality of individuality; the inequality of success; the glorious inequality of talent, of genius; for inequality, not mediocrity, individual superiority, not standardisation, is the measure of progress of the world.

How do you eat an elephant? One bite at a time.

Those who speak most of progress measure it by quantity and not by quality.

G. Santayana

Don't accept progress reports such as 'quite good', 'not bad' or similar. Always insist upon a positive and specific report.

The average man on the street needs to know more science today than the teachers knew a generation ago, just to be able to read his newspapers and magazines intelligently. Music, art – those possessions formerly of the fortunate few – now belong to the people. Whatever field of subject matter you name, its content and significance for modern living has doubled, trebled . . . in recent years.

A.J. Stoddard

It does not follow that change also means progress.

Unquestionably, there is progress. The average European pays out much more in taxes than he formerly got in wages.

If you don't make progress, you'll be going backwards.

We must go forward in sensible stages. No golfer will go from being a rabbit to being a scratch player in one giant step. Let us try to cut the handicap to, say, 20 or 18. Such a step is not too ambitious and the golfer will still be far from good – but at least progress will have been made.

MAS

The reasonable man adapts himself to the world. The unreasonable man persists in trying to adapt the world to himself. Therefore, all progress depends upon the unreasonable man.

George Bernard Shaw

The child plucks the fruit from a tree the grandfather planted.

Kim Woo-Choong

Nothing stands still. We progress or regress.

Jimmy Reid

You can't go back; go forward. Don't dream; act!

Morris West

This is not the end. It is not even the beginning of the end. But it is, perhaps, the end of the beginning.

Winston S. Churchill

It is rarely possible to carry the torch of progress through a crowd without singeing somebody's beard.

Joshua Bruyn

PUNCTUALITY

Punctuality is the politeness of princes.

Sir Alexander Stone

People count up the faults of those who keep them waiting.

Punctuality is something that if you have it, there's often no one around to share it with you.

H. Baker

I believe in punctuality, but it often makes me lonely.

E.V. Lucas

I consider unpunctuality to be a vile habit and all my life I have tried to break myself of it.

Winston S. Churchill

QUALITY

'Best' is not a measure of success in competition. 'Best' is a measure of quality.

I have the simplest tastes. I am always satisfied with the best.

Oscar Wilde

Whatsoever is rightly done, however humble, is noble.

Henry Royce

Our quest for quality, which is really a quest for success, starts with the individual players in the game. We must put to rest the notion that paying one's dues is a one-time affair. In fact, in today's business environment, paying one's dues simply entitles you to get back in line and pay again and again. Quality is a top-to-bottom proposition in organisations of all kinds, public and private, profit and non-profit.

Dr M. Mescon

Quality never comes cheaply.

If a man can make a better mousetrap, or preach a more convincing argument, then the world will beat a path to his door, even if he builds his house in the woods. Quality is paramount and genuine quality will always prevail in the end.

Ralph Waldo Emerson

Quality is not a thing. It is a result.

David Watt

We are what we repeatedly do. Excellence then, is not an act but a habit.

Aristotle

Quality is a fashion that never goes out of date.

The race for quality has no finish line.

Every job is a self-portrait of the person who did it. Autograph your work with excellence.

The quality of a person's life is in direct proportion to their commitment to excellence.

QUESTIONS

When I was a boy I used to do what my father wanted. Now I have to do what my son wants. My problem is: when am I going to do what I want to do?

Sam Levinson

The 'silly question' is the first intimation of some totally new development.

Alfred North Whitehead

It is a wise man who asks 'Why?'

Don't be afraid to ask 'What if?'

A band leader, who had played at over 2000 dances, was asked
'What have you had the most requests for?'
'Where's the men's room?' answered the maestro.

Bill Thorpe

Is anybody there? Does anybody care?

A young man once asked Mozart how to write a symphony.
Mozart said, 'You're very young, why not begin with ballads?'
The youth said, 'You composed symphonies when you were ten
years old.' 'Yes,' replied Mozart, 'but I didn't ask how.'

Useful prompts:
   Would you explain that to me?
   How do you feel about that?
   What would you have done?
   Why did you say that?
   For example?

If you're so clever, why aren't you rich?

If at first you don't succeed, ask yourself 'Why?'

Ask not what we say but what we do.

P.W. Bridgman

The only really dumb questions are the ones you do not have the
courage to ask.

Why are we having to do this?
What will be the consequences of our action?
What will happen if we stop?

Before asking questions for which you do not have the answers,
make a point of asking some questions to which you already
know the answers. If you receive correct answers to these
questions, you can have confidence in the responses to the other
questions.

Bryan K. Silver

When someone asks you a question you don't want to answer,
smile and ask 'Why do you want to know?'

Any question is easy when you know the answer.

QUITTING

When things go wrong, as they sometimes will,
When the road you're trudging seems all up hill,
When the funds are low and the debts are high,
And you want to smile, but you have to sigh,
When care is pressing you down a bit,
Rest, if you must – but don't you quit.

If all else fails, give up.

If at first you don't succeed, try, try again.
Then quit. No use being a damn fool about it.

W.C. Fields

Resignation is the courage of the impotent.

If you give in, you give up.

Winners never quit. Quitters never win.

Never, never quit. That is the coward's way out.

REACTIONS

It was just a suggestion, but he jumped at it like a trout taking a fly at twilight.

Animals react; people think . . . except when people react without thinking and then they are behaving like animals.

REALITY

Accept the realisation that slaves are not innovators and serfs cannot effectively service modern industry.

The world is like a mirror; it reflects the face you show it.

Reality is a foreign land – they do things differently there.

We can no longer afford an obsolete society of obsolete people.
H.K. Morse

Education is an admirable thing but it is well to remember that the realities of life cannot be taught; they must be learned . . . the hard way.
Oscar Wilde

Everything takes longer, costs more, and is less useful.
Erwin Tomash

The real world comes as a nasty surprise.

The world is full of people who play at life and only discover reality when it kicks them in the teeth.

Tom Sharpe

Let us bring reality into their lives; let's pay them in their own coin.

The sun shines on the righteous . . . and also on the unworthy, the ungodly and the unjust.

Reality bites, in the end, and it is biting now.

Paul Hayward

Reality is messy.

Sometimes reality just has to rear its ugly head.

In nature there are neither rewards nor punishments; there are consequences.

Robert Ingersoll

The reason tough decisions are called tough is because they are not easy.

Grow up. We're talking about life, death and the hereafter. No one gets an absolution from reality.

Morris West

REASONING

When you have eliminated the impossible, whatever remains, however improbable, must be the truth.

Sir Arthur Conan Doyle

In any given situation, think of all the possibilities. It's called looking for the fifth side of a square.

Bryan K. Silver

Do not look to where you fell but to where you slipped.

REASONS

Ask in any village what is the greatest concern, police officers claim, and you will be told it is speeding motorists rather than burglars. Cynics may suspect that the real reason is that errant motorists are easier to catch than burglars.

Geoffrey Wheatcroft

Reasons before the fact are predictions; and reasons after the fact are what astronomers call 'noise' – sounds that don't signify.

We have a reason for living, and a price for dying.

We may end up doing the right thing, but for quite the wrong reasons.

RECREATION

As manpower is replaced by other sources of energy the entire conception of recreation shifts. What we do with these new leisure hours will determine the value of our culture.

Morris Ernst

How beautiful it is to do nothing; and then rest afterwards.

RELATIVITY

But it's no use our playing noughts and crosses while the rest of the world is playing chess.

Why not to touch? One finger touching may not seem like much but a million fingers will touch an exhibit out of existence.

Good and bad men are each less so than they seem.

S.T. Coleridge

The world is full of checks and balances. Just when you get to the point where menu prices don't matter, calories do.

Phil Harris

A molehill is a mountain to the apprentice skier.

An insect in the bedroom is not quite the same as an insect in the garden.

There were two hunters in the woods. They came round a bend and there facing them was a huge grizzly bear. One of the hunters reached into his knapsack, pulled out a pair of trainers, and started putting them on as quickly as he could. The other hunter said, 'What are you doing that for? You can't outrun a grizzly.' The first hunter said 'I don't have to outrun the grizzly. I only have to outrun you.' Everything is relative.

As the man said when he jumped off the Empire State building and passed the twentieth floor, 'So far, so good.'

There are no shadows in a dark street.

And as ye sow, so shall ye reap.

We would do well to remember that the commonplace items of three or four hundred years ago are the precious antiques and art treasures of today.

J.K. Jerome

It is not so important to know where we stand, but rather to know if we are moving and if so, in what direction.

The difference between a pat on the back and a kick in the pants is barely eighteen inches.

Leonard Caulton

When a man sits with a pretty girl for an hour, it seems like a minute. But let him sit on a hot stove for a minute and it's longer than any hour. That's relativity.

Albert Einstein

RELIGION

Any religious leader whose community does not disagree with him, even in some small measure, is not really a teacher.

When a man says he can get by without religion it merely means that he has a kind of religion that he can get on without.

To be a man of the church is not always to be a man of God.

C. Cahier

Fanatics who suffer from religion, instead of enjoying it.

Infidel: In New York, one who does not believe in the Christian religion; in Constantinople, one who does.

Ambrose Bierce

Confess your sins to the Lord and you will be forgiven; confess them to man and you will be laughed at.

Josh Billings

All religions issue Bibles against Satan, and say the most injurious things against him, but we never hear his side.

Mark Twain

Christian: One who believes that the New Testament is a divinely inspired book, admirably suited to the spiritual needs of his neighbour.

Ambrose Bierce

There is no such thing as an atheist in an open boat.

There are few atheists before a battle.

John Blashford-Snell

All religions are dedicated to male supremacy. The men spend all their time thinking about complex theological problems, while their women sweep the floor for them, cook their food and have their babies.

Len Deighton

Compassion for all creatures is the only true religion.

We have just enough religion to make us hate, but not enough to make us love one another.

Swift

Religion is the opium of the masses.

Church history is always written to justify the survivors.

Morris West

An atheist is a man who has no invisible means of support.

John Buchan

REPUTATION

I have never understood this adulation of Moses. I calculate that in the forty years he wandered about the desert, not knowing his ass from his elbow, he could have accomplished great things. For example, if he had led his people just thirty yards a day in the right direction, he would have landed them not in Israel but in England, and all this confusion would have been avoided.

Character is what a man is. Reputation may be what he is not.

The best way to benefit from a good reputation is just to keep doing the things that earned it for you in the first place. That's not a bad way to lead a life, or run a business.

You can't build a reputation on what you're going to do.

RESISTANCE TO CHANGE

You can always tell a Harvard man, but you can't tell him much.

There is nothing more difficult to take in hand, more perilous to conduct or more uncertain in its success, than to take the lead in the introduction of a new order of things; because the innovator has for enemies all those who have done well under the old conditions, and lukewarm defenders in those who might do well under the new.

Machiavelli

People waste far more emotional energy desperately hanging on to old habits and beliefs than it would take for them to embrace the changes.

Price Pritchett, Ron Pound

Many people make the mistake of trying harder instead of trying differently. Trying harder won't take you very far if you're failing to do the right things. 'More of the same' may just add stress and tension.

Price Pritchett, Ron Pound

If you think adapting is tough duty, just see how difficult life becomes if you don't.

Price Pritchett, Ron Pound

RESOLVE

We must WANT to see things better; not just SAY that things should be better.

We need to abandon our passion for an ancient set of values that places great emphasis on continuity, security and sophistication, that exalts time-honoured good form in a sinking ship. We need to be a coarser, more vigorous, more hard-nosed, more determined society. In other words, we need to be in peace what we have always been in war.

Brian Walden

Don't say 'If only'; say 'Next time.'

Too often we are scared. Scared of what we might not be able to do. Scared of what people might think if we tried. We let our fears stand in the way of our hopes. We say 'no' when we want to say 'yes'. We sit quietly when we want to scream. And we shout with the others when we should keep quiet. Why? After all, we only go round once. There's really no time to be afraid. So stop. Try something you've never tried. Risk it. Write a letter to the editor. Demand a raise. Scrap your TV. Speak out. Travel where you don't speak the language. Call her. You've nothing to lose and everything to gain. JUST DO IT.

Nothing ever built rose to touch the skies unless some man dreamed that it should, some man believed that it could, and some man willed that it must.

I like to get things right and I don't give up.

Kevin Leech

Some succeed because they are destined to, but most succeed because they are determined to.

RESPECT

This is the final test of a gentleman: his respect for those who can be of no possible service to him.

W.L. Phelps

To be capable of respect is almost as rare as to be worthy of it.

Joseph Joubert

Respect cannot be demanded, or bought; it must be earned.

Knowing how to hide your grief is no more than respect for other people.

Jacques Chirac

Politicians, ugly buildings and whores all become respectable if they last long enough.

The true measure of a man's achievement in life is not how well he is liked, but how well he is respected. If you buy enough beer for people or give lots of money to charity, you will be liked; being respected is quite different.

Remember the three Rs: Respect for self; Respect for others; Responsibility for all your actions.

RESPONSIBILITY

Responsibility must be shouldered; you cannot carry it under your arm.

The price of power is responsibility for the public good.
W.W. Aldrich

Restricting the opportunities in literature and numeracy will ensure that future generations have to carry a terrible burden of inability, ignorance and disadvantage.

You can't depend on the man who made the mess to clean it up.
Richard M. Nixon

The best person to decide what research work shall be done is the man who is doing the research, and the next best person is the head of the department, who knows all about the subject and the work. After that you leave the field of the best people and start on increasingly worse groups, the first being the research director, who is probably wrong more than half the time; and then a committee, which is wrong most of the time; and finally, a committee of vice-presidents of the Company, which is wrong all the time.
Dr. Mees

The only way to get rid of responsibilities is to discharge them.

Walter S. Robertson

Freedom of speech does not imply freedom from responsibility.

REVENGE

To punish in anger amounts to taking revenge.

Revenge is a dish best eaten cold.

Angelo Fusco

Revenge is sweet, but not fattening.

Never kick a man when he is down: that is supposed to be the rule of a gentleman. How ridiculous. There is not a better moment to put the boot in.

Minette Marrin

Nemo me impune lacessit . . . Nobody provokes me with impunity.

Nothing is more costly, nothing is more sterile, than vengeance.

Winston S. Churchill

Before setting out on revenge, dig two graves.

RICHES

A man is rich in proportion to the number of things which he can afford to let alone.

H.D. Thoreau

If capital has to be used to any extent, remember that no really rich man ever puts his own money at risk if he can help it.

David Moreau

It is better to live rich, than to die rich.

Samuel Johnson

There are people who have nothing of their fortune except the fear of losing it.

Every day I get up and look through the Forbes list of the richest people in America. If I'm not there, I go to work.

Robert Orben

The rich can afford the time to be ill.

RIGHTS

America – a place where the people have the right to complain about the lack of freedom.

L. Hirsch

We need a return to decorum, manners and the rights of the community as opposed to individual rights. We have just about reached the limits of individualism. It's time to turn down the volume and think of the community.

Willard Gaylin

Every right has its corresponding duty.

The meek shall inherit the earth; but not the mineral rights.

Those who are quick to claim their rights are often slow to do their duty.

A driving licence is not a right; it's a privilege.

There's too much of an entitlement attitude nowadays. 'I deserve this' needs to be replaced with 'I earned this.'

Michael Dell

Citizenship involves duties and obligations as well as rights.

People do not value a right until it is taken away.

George Bernard Shaw

Pioneers get the arrows; settlers get the land.

RUDENESS

Rudeness is the weak man's imitation of strength.

Whoever one is, and wherever one is, one is always in the wrong if one is rude.

He was born rude and badly brought up.

Observation of a person at a dance: 'The swamp is empty. All the monsters are here.'

Harry Harris

RULES

It is a basic rule never to waste anything, be it time or scraps of paper.

G.C. Lichtenberg

You learn the rules by study, and the exceptions to the rules by experience.

In a well ordered society, the vast majority of rules should be used as signposts and not as fences. They should provide guidance rather than restriction.

MAS

There's no rule without an exception.

A rule broken by practically everyone in the firm soon becomes the new rule.

The Golden Rule is that he who has the gold makes the rules. The Power Rule is that he who has the power makes the rules.

If the ruler sets a good example, the people will be easy to manage.

Confucius

RUMOUR

I won't go into details, I've already told you more than I heard myself.

H. Martin

Rumours of ill spread like wildfire; rumours of good are as a dying fire.

I rarely repeat gossip, so listen very carefully.

There are a number of rumours around and as rumour feeds on itself, this could cause unnecessary trouble.

If you haven't got anything nice to say about anybody, come and
sit next to me.

Alice Roosevelt Longworth

SADNESS

No man ever does a thing for the last time without a feeling of
sadness.

He never made anyone unhappy until he went away.

Tribute to Will Rogers

Maudlin is all right when you're by yourself, or between
consenting adults.

William Ronald Miller

Talk about sad. He spends his waking hours dragging his spirit
through a barrel of treacle.

Do not show your sadness to others.

Jacques Chirac

SATISFACTION

The crowning fortune of a man is to be born to some pursuit
which finds him employment and happiness, whether it be to
make baskets or broadswords, or canals, or statues, or songs.

Ralph Waldo Emerson

When our best friends are in trouble, there is always the
something that is not wholly displeasing to us.

La Rochefoucauld

It is said that for true happiness it is not enough to succeed oneself. It is also necessary for one's closest friends to fail.

Minette Marrin

It was splendid whenever I conquered my desires but when I failed it was a pleasure too.

Marjorie Phillips

SCIENCE

The final test of science is not whether its accomplishments add to our comfort, knowledge and power, but whether it adds to our dignity as men, our sense of truth and beauty.
It is a test science cannot pass alone and unaided.

D. Sarnoff

In science the credit goes to the man who convinces the world, not to the man to whom the idea first occurs.

Sir W. Osler

Science is there to be used. It is not there to tell us how things are, and science is not powerful because it is true, but true because it is powerful.

The opposite of a correct statement is a false statement. But the opposite of a profound truth may well be another profound truth.

Niels Bohr

You cannot have a science without measurement.

R.W. Hamming

Hear the tale of Frederick Worms, whose parents weren't on speaking terms. So when Fred wrote to Santa Claus, he wrote in duplicate because one went to Dad and one to Mum, each asking for plutonium. So Frederick's father and his mother, without consulting one another, each bought a lump of largish size, intending it as a surprise, which met in Frederick's stocking and laid waste some ten square miles of land. Learn from this tale of nuclear fission, not to mix science and superstition.

Gilbert Harding

SECRETS

The curious are the worst keepers of secrets.

What two know is a secret; what three know is the latest news.

Three may keep a secret, if two of them are dead.

Benjamin Franklin

Never tell your friend a secret; remember that your friend has a friend.

The Talmud

The backbone of surprise is fusing speed with secrecy.

Von Clausewitz

SEEING

To see a thing once is better than hearing about it often.

Eyes make better witnesses than ears.

Originality is simply a pair of fresh eyes.

One sees great things from the valley; only small things from the peak.

G.K. Chesterton

No man is so blind as the man who will not see.

Jonathan Swift

Eyes believe themselves. Ears believe others.

People see what they have been conditioned to see; they refuse to see what they don't expect to see.

Merle P. Martin

Seeing ourselves as others see us wouldn't be much good. We wouldn't believe it, anyway.

Worth seeing? Yes; but not worth going to see.

Samuel Johnson

There are none so blind as those who will not see – except perhaps, those who refuse to look.

Hearing something one hundred times is not as good as seeing it once.

SELF-CONTROL

Consider how John Templeton, a child of the Great Depression and one of the smartest and wealthiest investors around, got his start. As an impoverished young man, Templeton vowed to save 50 per cent of his earnings, to refrain from all consumer borrowing, never to spend over 16 per cent of his income on renting shelter and to never take a home mortgage exceeding one-half of a year's income. Until he became a wealthy man, he never wavered from these rules.

Self-control is the mark of true civilization.

Resolve not to be poor; whatever you have, spend less.

The line between strong self-discipline and masochism can sometimes be very fine.

Complete self-control is eating one salted peanut.

Pam Friend

SELF-ESTEEM

People may differ in tradition, language and religion, but they all have one common denominator – a desire to be treated like human beings.

S.C. Allyn

There is something about saying 'OK' and hanging up the telephone receiver with a bang that kids a man into feeling that he has just pulled off a big deal, even if he has only called up the speaking clock to find out the correct time.

R. Benchley

Great people believe in themselves; small people want others to believe in them.

Lichtenberg

They call me a punk. But who gave them the right to put a label on me? Everyone has his price where he will sell out his principles. It's just that my price is lower than most.

Oh that we had some power to see ourselves as others see us!

Robert Burns

If you do not believe in yourself, the chances are that nobody else will.

Never be afraid of what 'they' say. 'They' exist only in your fears. What you do is the only thing that counts. What 'they' say means nothing.

Everybody needs a sense of identity.

SELF-INTEREST

Look alive! You could be replaced by a button.

Up with the drawbridge, Septimus; I am over the moat.

MAS

No institution will survive if it is dedicated only to self-preservation. A business is not a biological organism whose survival is a virtue in itself. Rather, it is a man-created institution, an integral part of our culture, and as such must make a contribution of service to society (as well as a profit for itself) if it hopes to survive. It cannot do this out of a focus on self-gain or pride.

Dr L. Finkelstein

In any controversy, the instant we feel anger we have already ceased striving for truth and have begun striving for ourselves.

The ultimate motivation has always been self-preservation.

Do unto others before they do unto you.

Give me the luxuries of life and I will willingly do without the necessities.

Frank Lloyd Wright

The matter was decided with due regard to logical necessity.

Doing a job right the first time gets the job done. Doing the job wrong fourteen times gives you job security.

SELF-PITY

Regret is an appalling waste of energy; you can't build on it, it's only good for wallowing in.

K. Mansfield

No pity is wasted except self-pity.

When you are sure that everything is going badly for you, remember the man who was complaining loudly that he had no shoes . . . and then he saw a man who had no feet.

You must never regret what might have been. The past that did not happen is as hidden from us as the future we cannot see.

Richard M. Stern

Don't yield to the seductive pull of self-pity.

Price Pritchett, Ron Pound

SELLING

A business exists for the purpose of making a profit. Everything depends on this because without profit there is no business, no employment and none of the many other considerations associated with commercial enterprises. In order to make a profit, a business must earn revenue; so the fundamental requirement of any business is to separate customers from their money. All other considerations are secondary to this. Until someone buys what you have to sell, be you shop keeper or teacher or brain surgeon, you have nothing.

MAS

If he tried to sell bread, people would probably stop eating.

Edith Saville

It is as much an art as a science to design a product that will sell. The successful corporation is the one that masters the art as well as the science.

F. Donner

'Marketing' is the process of anticipating, specifying and satisfying the future needs of customers.

David Coats

No sale is a good sale for Neiman–Marcus unless it is a good buy for the customer.

Herbert Marcus

Thermal incentive scheme . . . if you don't sell you're fired!

Salesmanship is the art of teaching people to want what you have to sell.

The difference between, say, a computer salesman and a used car salesman is that the used car salesman knows when he is not telling the truth.

David Watt

Making your quota gives you the right to complain.

Stan Bootle

Your job is to win orders – not to win arguments.

Stan Bootle

You sell the sizzle before you sell the steak.

SENSE OF PROPORTION

Don't forget: more competitions are lost than won.

There is nothing wrong with having toys, as long as we retain the sense of proportion to recognise them as such.

It's not so much about what you've got to lose, it's about what you've got to gain.

It's all very well living in a beautiful part of the country; but can you earn a living, do the facilities exist to give you the quality of life that you want? You can't eat scenery.

Look not at what you have lost, but at what you have left.

We need to abandon the expendables, because that creates valuable space.

Price Pritchett, Ron Pound

Some people waste too much emotional energy fighting over trivial issues. They blow things out of proportion, giving major attention to minor problems. For these people, practically no issue is so small that it merits being ignored.

Price Pritchett, Ron Pound

The colour of the cat is unimportant provided it catches mice.

Deng Xiaoping

The poacher who shoots at rabbits may scare away the big game.

THE GLASGOW HERALD SYNDROME

Don't let your ambitions be hidden from the light of reason. Your presses can print 80,000 copies per day but you know you could sell another 15,000 copies. Your ambitions cause you to install new presses and you do sell 95,000 copies. However, the new presses could print 150,000 copies so although your sales have gone up your operating costs have also risen steeply and your profitability has decreased. The price of more sales could be less profit. Have a care.

MAS

SEXUALITY

Economists are still trying to work out why the girl with the least principles draws the most interest.

G. Black

In the old days, if you wanted to know if a girl had knock-knees you had to listen.

Vic Damone

A low neckline is something you can look down upon and approve of at the same time.

It must be discouraging to a sensible girl when she observes the way sensible men smile at silly girls.

S. Jones

A woman's chief asset is a man's imagination.

If you make love as slowly as you eat, I'd like to get to know you better.

After dinner gambit

There is one form of life to which I unconditionally surrender, which is the female gender.

Ogden Nash

Sex is an itch that must be scratched.

It is now possible for a flight attendant to get a pilot pregnant.

Richard J. Ferris

SILENCE

Beware of the silent man and a dog that does not bark.

It's a wise man who holds his tongue when he is right.

Sometimes one must remain silent to be heard.

It is better to keep your mouth shut and be thought a fool than open it and remove all doubt.

Heinrich Heine

A closed mouth gathers no foot.

R.E. Wilson

Blessed is the man who has nothing to say and cannot be persuaded to say it.

Speech may sometimes do harm; but so may silence, and a worse harm at that. No offered insult ever caused so deep a wound as a tenderness expected and withheld; and no spoken indiscretion was ever so bitterly regretted as the words one did not speak.

Silence is a fine jewel for a woman but it is little worn.

To say nothing often reflects a fine command of the English language.

When you have nothing to say, say nothing.

Silence is the most perfect expression of scorn.
George Bernard Shaw

Silence is not only golden; it is seldom misquoted.
Bob Monkhouse

You are never sorry for what you never said.
Benjamin Disraeli

Well-timed silence has more eloquence than speech.
Martin Farquhar Tupper

The drumming silence of the country on the ears of the town dweller.

SINCERITY

The merit of originality is not novelty: it is sincerity.
Thomas Carlyle

If you really want peace, you have to declare war on revenge.
Ernest Levy

When you say 'I'm sorry', look the person in the eye.

SOLDIERS

Soldiers fight, but kings become heroes.

Those who make peaceful revolution impossible will make
violent revolution inevitable.

John F. Kennedy

Man is a military animal; glories in gunpowder and loves
parades.

P.J. Bailey

Soldiers who wish to be a hero
Are practically zero;
But those who wish to be civilians,
Jesus, they run into the millions.

We are the unwilling . . . led by the unqualified . . . to do the
unnecessary . . . for the ungrateful . . .

GI in Vietnam, 1970

Old soldiers never die. Young ones do.

Violence is the last refuge of the incompetent.

Azimov

SOUNDS

If the crow could feed in quiet, he would have more meat.

Horace

You never realise how the human voice can change until a woman stops nagging her husband to answer the telephone.

Acoustic wallpaper; the sound of so-called Hi Fi.

Ivor Tiefenbrun

SPEECH

Put brain in gear before opening mouth.

If you speak three languages, you are trilingual.
If you speak two languages, you are bilingual.
If you speak only one language, you are British.

When there is nothing more to be said, be sure some silly fellow says it.

People don't remember jokes, they remember style, the general impression.

The safe way to qualify any statement: 'Without prejudice or commitment.'

After dinner speaking is an occupation monopolised by men – women can't wait that long.

S. Miller

The best of spontaneous remarks requires very careful rehearsal.

A word and a stone, once launched, cannot be recalled.

Those with too much to say end up with too small an audience.

Speak quietly, but carry a big stick.

No one should speak more clearly than they think.

Alfred North Whitehead

He has the gift of compressing the largest amount of words into the smallest amount of thought.

Winston S. Churchill

I quote others only the better to express myself.

Michel de Montaigne

Don't talk about yourself; the others will, after you've gone.

Talking and eloquence are not the same; to speak and to speak well are two different things.

Ben Jonson

Nothing needs more preparation than the impromptu.

'In closing' is always followed by the other half of the speech.

The purpose of language is twofold, to communicate emotion and to give information.

Aldous Huxley

The last word ever spoken will probably be 'Why?'

The nice thing about egotists is that they don't talk about other people.

Lucille S. Harper

STATISTICS

Statistics are like bikinis . . . what they reveal may be interesting but what they conceal is fascinating.

A single death is a tragedy, a million deaths is a statistic.

Stalin

There are three kinds of men; liars, damn liars and statisticians.

Modern reports are a case of more information, but fewer specific conclusions and recommendations.

Reliability engineering is based upon the branch of mathematics laughingly known as statistics. If you lay all the statisticians in the world end to end, they will still point in all directions.

William Ronald Miller

STATUS

What people say behind your back is the true measure of your standing in the community.

'You are a bastard.'

'Correct, and in my case, an accident of birth; but you're a self-made man.'

Just because nobody disagrees with you does not necessarily mean you are brilliant – maybe you're the boss.

J. Holmes

The man who is denied the opportunity of taking decisions of importance begins to regard as important the decisions he is allowed to take. He becomes fussy about filing, keen on seeing the pencils are sharpened, eager to ensure that the windows are open (or shut) and apt to use two or three different-coloured inks.

C. Northcote Parkinson

Either you are a manipulator, or you are manipulated.

It is difficult to esteem a man as highly as he would wish.

Vauvenargues

STRENGTH

The tree falls not at the first stroke.

Don't ask for a light burden – ask for a strong back.

Do not pray for an easy life. Pray to be a strong person.

A good beginning makes you twice as strong.

To achieve what you want, you have to be stronger than those around you.

Benjamin Disraeli

'Who do you think you are?'
'What does it matter; I'm bigger than you.'

Kick their ass first, then negotiate with your foot on their neck.

General George S. Patton

True strength lies in having the courage to do the right thing.

Kazuo Inamori

It's not the size of the dog in the fight, it's the size of the fight in the dog.

Mark Twain

STRENGTH OF CHARACTER

If you can't stand the heat, get out of the kitchen.

Harry S. Truman

By the time I left school an important principle had begun to penetrate my brain. That was that life is a stern struggle and a boy has to be able to stand up to the buffeting. There are many attributes which he must acquire to succeed. Two are vital: hard work and absolute integrity.

Lord Montgomery

Faced with crisis, the man of character falls back upon himself. He imposes his own stamp on action, takes responsibility for it, makes it his own. Difficulty attracts the man of character because it is in embracing it that he realises himself.

Charles de Gaulle

I don't want any pardon for what I've done, or am.

Confederate Civil War song

He who does not bellow the truth when he knows the truth makes himself the accomplice of liars and forgers.

The superior man does not wrangle.
He is firm but not quarrelsome.

Impose yourself: the lions have to know that the lion tamer has arrived.

Sir Lewis Robertson

A professional is someone who can do his best work when he doesn't feel like it.

Alistair Cooke

I may be only one person, but I can be one person who makes a difference.

Vadra Groce

Don't let your neighbour set your standards. Be yourself.

Robert Louis Stevenson

The truly great man is not soured by lack of recognition.

Confucius

A man does what he must – in spite of personal consequences, in spite of obstacles and dangers and pressures – and that is the basis of all human morality.

John F. Kennedy

Fortunately my back is broad enough to disregard completely the opinions of those I have no regard for.

Marjorie Phillips

It's easy to do anything in victory – it's in defeat that a man reveals himself.

Floyd Patterson

STRESS

Is it so essential to acquire more capital/pension before you retire? I have known too many friends and acquaintances who died as a result of stress and hassle. I do not know of anyone who died from hunger or cold.

MAS

Life is like a piece of stick, which represents a person's life expectancy. Nobody knows the length of their piece of stick but whenever you are involved in a really stressful situation, regardless of whether you win or lose, a minuscule shaving is removed from the stick. There are umpteen ways to shorten the stick but, so far, I have never learned how to lengthen it. Every hassle, every serious, contentious argument, all succeed in shortening the stick. Simple unhappiness or disappointment are not stick-shortening. Consider the price you may pay before you go into a possible stick-shortening situation.

MAS

STUPIDITY

Ignorant is for now, but stupid is forever.

You're supposed to be stupid; don't abuse the privilege!

.... is the apex of stupidity.

I don't object to your being a bastard, but your being such a stupid bastard is what I do object to.

There is no sin except stupidity.

Oscar Wilde

Behaving as though stupidity was a virtue.

The detestable smell of stupidity.

Everyone can make a mistake; to repeat it is stupidity.

The most costly of all follies is to believe passionately in the palpably not true. It is the chief occupation of mankind.

H.L. Mencken

Someone with the brains of a plant.

Someone with the brains of an empty lemonade bottle.

We are surrounded by a deep and abiding stupidity.

Bob Herbert

Robin Hood was a fool. He should have kept the money for the rich. They would have known what to do with it.

Sir Sacheverell Sitwell

A sinner can repent but stupid is forever.

He had a firm grasp of the wrong end of the stick, and a clear view of the inessential.

A fool and his words are soon parted.

William Shenstone

Against stupidity, the Gods themselves battled in vain.

Only two things are infinite, the universe and human stupidity; and I'm not sure about the former.

Albert Einstein

Artificial Intelligence is no match for Natural Stupidity.

SUCCESS

Behind every successful man stands a completely amazed mother-in-law.

Lord Wheatley

Good fortune is never good until it is lost.

The man who is best provided with information has the most success in life.

Every success is founded on numerous failures.

No crime is so great as daring to excel.

Success in life depends upon the three 'I's: Integrity, Intelligence and Industry.

Charles R. Stockard

Success has a simple formula: do your best, and people may like it.

The moment of victory is much too short to live for, and nothing else.

Martina Navratilova

He made his money the really old-fashioned way; he inherited it.

Success is a journey, not a destination.

The secret of success is to know something nobody else knows.

Aristotle Onassis

SUFFICIENCY

Three things are good in little measure and evil in large: yeast, salt and hesitation.

The Talmud

You don't know what enough is until you've had too much.

The rich man is no happier than the man who has enough.

Solon

The poor have little, beggars none:
The rich too much; enough . . . not one.

You can't collect all the beautiful pebbles on the beach.

Pick the flowers, but spare the buds.

There will never be enough of everything while the world goes on. The more that is given the more there will be needed.

Winston S. Churchill

SUPPORT

To keep from falling is better than to hold up.

I may not be best butter, but I'm on your side of the bread.

A helping hand is worth more than a thousand words of advice.

Small deeds are worth more than big words.

There is nothing but wind in a pneumatic tyre, yet it eases wonderfully the jolts along life's highway.

Marshal Foch

You have my hand to hold, and it will only be released if you let it go.

Brian Lever

A bit of help is worth a great of pity.

Hilda Turner

225

SURVIVAL

It is difficult to think nobly when one thinks only to get a living.

How cruel life is; the endless chase just to fill our stomachs.

War doesn't decide who is right or wrong – only who survives.

He may be down, but he's not out.

Every morning in Africa, a gazelle wakes up. It knows it must run faster than the fastest lion or it will be killed. Every morning a lion wakes up. It knows it must outrun the slowest gazelle or it will starve to death. It doesn't matter whether you are a lion or a gazelle . . . when the sun comes up you'd better be running.

Only those who adapt to change survive.

Charles Darwin

Survival isn't necessarily a comfortable process. But it sure beats the alternative.

Price Pritchett, Ron Pound

It is not too hard to be young without money, but it is very difficult being old without it.

Tennessee Williams

SYMPATHY

Sympathy is the gift of knowing without being told.

One of the finest and truest definitions of sympathy is: 'Sympathy is your pain in my heart.'

H.E. Luccock

226

We've got to ration our sympathy in this world; we have only so much to give.

Sympathy without relief is like mustard without beef.

SYSTEMS

If the manual disciplines are bad, the computer will be a waste of money.

MAS

I am in accord with the system, so long as it permits me to function effectively.

Documentation is like sex: when it is good, it is very, very good; and when it is bad, it is better than nothing.

Dick Brandon

The system works fine, except in a case like this, where it seems foolish.

Harold Ross

The fault lies not with our technologies but with our systems.

Levian

This business runs on the 'eventually' basis. Eventually our systems tell us whatever we want to know, but by the time we get the information it is often too late to do anything about it.

Ian Carlaw

Whenever a new system or procedure is introduced, it is essential that use of the new system is the only way to accomplish a particular task. The planning for the new system must ensure, therefore, the utter non-availability of any earlier methods for carrying out the work.

MAS

TACT

The art of being wise is the art of knowing what to overlook.

The most effective command is the one made to sound like a request.

Tact is the ability to describe others as they see themselves.

Tact is, after all, a kind of mind-reading.

Tact is the ability to keep silent at the right moment.

TAXATION

Nowadays when your ship comes in, the Inland Revenue sees it is safely docked.

Inheritance Tax is, broadly speaking, a voluntary levy paid by those who distrust their heirs more than they distrust the Inland Revenue.

Lord Jenkins

TEACHING

The Japanese now take the view that, with the right educational methods, a child can master virtually any subject – if the child really wants to do so. The revolutionary Suzuki method of teaching the violin was in fact the first application of this new thinking. We all thought – or I certainly thought – children had to be potential prodigies to play the violin at all. Not so, apparently.

The most important unsolved problem in education is discovering and releasing the maximum potential of each child. We need poets, senators, businessmen, as well as scientists and engineers. If we discover what children have in them early enough, we'll have more than enough of everything.

John Hersey

The best teacher is willing to be forgotten. His only reassurance needs to be the faith that somehow his efforts have increased the amount of mind in a world which can never have too much of that commodity. His final reward is the quality of life, which his teaching has helped to shape.

Mark Van Doren

The possibility of succeeding even occasionally in getting students to want to develop fully their intellectual powers is more wonderful to me than the possibility of launching any number of space machines.

J. Harris

Give a man a fish, and you feed him for a day.
Teach a man to fish, and you feed him for a lifetime.

A good teacher can open a door but you must go through it with your own efforts.

TEAMWORK

Coming together is a beginning; keeping together is progress; working together is success.

The vehicle of accomplishment is fuelled by teamwork.

Together everyone achieves more.

Teamwork is the ability to work together towards a common vision, the ability to direct individual accomplishment towards organisational objectives. Teamwork is the fuel that allows common people to attain uncommon results.

TECHNOLOGY

The future lies in showing people how to use technology. If we do not show them, they're not going to use it.

Joan Berkman

Never forget that technology is a tool for people, rather than vice versa.

TEENAGE YEARS

A juvenile delinquent is a teenager who wants what he wants when he wants it and won't wait to get it.

C.F. Murphy

Heredity is what makes the mother and father of teenagers wonder a little about each other.

G.L. Hull

It seems to be an immutable law of human nature that each new generation will dress, speak, make love, and listen to music in the way best calculated to infuriate their elders.

Every teenager discovers at some moment or other that his parents are sometimes right.

The modern teenager oscillates between superb optimism and the self-destruct mode.

William Ronald Miller

Few things are more satisfying than seeing your children have teenagers of their own.

Teenagers, if you are tired of being hassled by unreasonable parents, now is the time for action. Leave home and pay your own way while you still know everything.

TELEVISION

Television is a device that enables people who haven't anything to do to watch people who can't do anything.

F. Allen

If you've been watching the TV commercials, you get the impression that Venus de Milo must have used too harsh a detergent.

P. Moody

Before television, nobody even knew what a headache looked like.

D. Fields

Chewing gum for the eyes – mediocre films/TV shows.

Day-time television is a life-support system for the over 60s and the unemployed.

TEMPTATION

The only way to get rid of a temptation is to yield to it.

Oscar Wilde

THINKING

Companies and places that are growing are growing by inno-vating a great deal, by thinking a great deal. Look upon this as 'thoughtware' economy because it is so heavily based on thinking.

One man likes to say what he knows, another what he thinks.

Joseph Joubert

You can lead a man up to the university, but you can't make him think.

When all else fails, try thinking.

You need to be able to think simply in order to achieve complicated things.

Think wrongly, if you please, but in all cases think for yourself.

Knowing is no substitute for thinking.

Of course I thought. I just thought wrongly.

Elaine Silver

THRIFT

Misers are no fun to live with, but as ancestors they are great.

No one admires thrift more than an heir.

Saving is a very fine thing. Especially when your parents have done it for you.

Winston S. Churchill

TIME

Three o'clock is always too late or too early for anything you want to do.

Jean-Paul Sartre

As we advance in time, we acquire a keener sense of the value of time. Nothing else, indeed, seems of any consequence; and we become misers in this respect.

Hazlitt

The trouble with morning is that it comes at such an ungodly hour.

Lose an hour in the morning and you will spend all day looking for it.

The sooner the 'was' the better.

Running all the way doesn't help much; the thing to do is to start out on time.

It takes less time to do a thing right than it does to explain why you did it wrong.

Longfellow

Be prepared to take a little longer to get it right. Remember the project manager who said, 'Why is it that we never have time to get it right – so we get it wrong three times?'

The Bird of Time has but a little way to fly – and Lo! the Bird is on the Wing.

Omar Khayyam

We all find time to do what we really want to do.

Weekends are a bit like rainbows; they look good from a distance but disappear when you get up close to them.

J. Shirley

The most valuable commodity in the world is time. Like an arrow from a bow, it never returns.

Kim Woo-Choong

Yesterday is history and tomorrow is just a vision, but today's a bitch.

Time is the ultimate commodity and you are born with only so much to spend; and nobody ever knows the exact amount.

Tom Clancy

Plagiarism saves time.

TOLERANCE

He may not suffer fools gladly, but he has to endure contact with a good many.

With all respect, I want, yea demand, to be taken seriously. I neither need nor want tolerance.

Your friend and your tooth; suffer them till death.

It is easy to be tolerant when you do not care.

TRAINING

Training is not a luxury; it is an investment.

Training is everything; cauliflower is nothing but cabbage with a college education.

Mark Twain

TRAVEL

There are far better places than a train for talk, but few places are a train's equal for reading.

J.M. Brown

The ideal place for a picnic is usually a little further on.

A stroll is a roundabout way of arriving at a pub.

Wim Kan

You have to travel far before you discover your own country.

The road to ruin is always in good repair, and the travellers pay the expense of it.

Josh Billings

If you can find a path with no obstacles, it probably doesn't lead anywhere.

If you are ever going to cross a desert on your own, it is essential to carry a pack of playing cards with you, as your insurance in case you get lost. If that happens, and you are hopelessly lost and don't know which way to go, just sit down, get out your cards and start playing patience. Inevitably, someone will come up behind you to say something like 'Black six on red seven' . . . and you will be rescued.

Travelling abroad is leaving your own country in order to grow more fond of it.

The journey is never over until the arrival.

Travel first class; if you don't, your children will.

When going abroad, take twice as much money and half as much clothing as you think you will need.

The man who goes alone can start today; but he who travels with another must wait until that other is ready.

H.D. Thoreau

TREASON

There is no such thing as a small treason.

TROUBLES

Trouble that is recognised is half cured.

It is always best not to tell people your troubles. Half of them are not interested, and the other half are glad you are getting what's coming to you.

When trouble goes to sleep, don't set the alarm clock.

When you're in trouble, let your partner play the hand.

Steve Walker

The most trouble is produced by those who don't produce anything.

Don't tell me your troubles, I've got troubles of my own.

Folk song

Don't borrow trouble. Imaginary things are harder to bear than the actual ones.

Robert Louis Stevenson

When troubles come, they come not as single spies but as whole battalions.

If it has tyres or testicles, it will cause trouble.

TRUST

When a man assumes a public trust, he should consider himself as public property.

Thomas Jefferson

I have seen flowers come in stony places
And kind things done by men with ugly faces,
And the gold cup won by the worst horse at the races,
So I trust, too.

John Masefield

You may rely on people with whom children and dogs make friends.

To be trusted is a greater compliment than to be loved.

When J. Edgar Hoover announced that no respectable citizen could trust men who wore long hair and beards, Claude told the local Associated Press man, 'Well, that takes care of Jesus Christ and Ulysses S. Grant.'

TRUTH

Truth is a fixed star.

Truth, like oil, will come to the surface at last.

When in doubt, tell the truth.

It is not always the right time to speak the truth.

The truth is the best remedy for slander.

Abraham Lincoln

An aphorism is never exactly true; it is either a half-truth or one-and-a-half truths.

Karl Kraus

The truth is a rabbit in a bramble patch.

Pete Seeger

Truth has no special time of its own. Its hour is now . . . always.

Albert Schweitzer

El momento de la verdad . . . the moment of truth.

Beware of a half-truth; you may have got hold of the wrong half.

The truth is more important than the facts.

Frank Lloyd Wright

Fraud and falsehood dread examination. Truth invites it.

Thomas Cooper

Truth is durable and it lasts; and it will come out eventually.

You can never bury the truth so deep that it can't be dug up.

And so a new layer of soil fell on the grave of truth.

The truth always hurts.

Celia Silver

Truth is the first casualty of any engagement in the battle of life.

Michael Green

It doesn't matter what the truth is; what matters is people's perception of the truth.

Simon Hume

Truth may tend at times to be dull yet it has a way of prevailing in the end.

Truth is too precious to tell every fool who asks for it.

UNDERSTANDING

In the matter of deep understanding, there is an important difference between simply knowing the name of something and really knowing something.

Richard Feynman

UPBRINGING

Any child who gets raised by the book must be a first edition.

D.S. Mowatt

Children cannot be expected to understand unless you instruct them and control their actions.

Beth Hatefutsoth

There's no such thing as bad children or bad dogs; there are bad parents and bad owners.

Aldo Farina

Bring up a child in the way that he should go, and when he is old he will not depart from it.

Trevor McDonald

The most influential of all educational factors is the conversation in a child's home.

Archbishop William Temple

USELESSNESS

He does the work of two men: Laurel and Hardy!

Mike Payne

His standard of performance could be compared to that of banjo players and comic singers, but have a care; maybe you are being rude to banjo players and comic singers?

He would be out of his depth in a car park puddle.

He has the wisdom of youth, and the energy of old age.

He should go far – and the sooner he starts, the better.

UTILIZATION

To a brave man, good and bad luck are like his right and left hand. He uses both.

St Catherine of Siena

VISION

Where there is no vision, the people perish.

Proverbs 29:18

Every man takes the limits of his own field of vision for the limits of the world.

Schopenhauer

Competence, like truth, beauty, and contact lenses, is in the eye of the beholder.

Dr Laurence J. Peter

I've seen the future, baby, and it's murder.

Leonard Cohen

Unless you're the lead dog, the scenery never changes.

Some men see things as they are and ask 'Why?' I dream things that never were and say 'Why not?'

George Bernard Shaw

VOTING

A straw vote only shows which way the hot air blows.

O'Henry

Scarcely anything has been pronounced by one learned person the contrary of which has not been asserted by one other; and it would avail nothing to count votes . . . for in the matter of a difficult question, it is far more likely that the truth should have been discovered by few than by many.

René Descartes

WAR

Once is happenstance; twice is coincidence; three times is organised warfare.

Ian Fleming

Revolutionaries who take the law into their own hands are horrifying not because they are criminals, but because they are like machines that have got out of control, like runaway trains.

Boris Pasternak

War is always a temporary misunderstanding.

Wim Kan

There never was a good war or a bad peace.

Benjamin Franklin

War hath no fury like a non-combatant.

Charles Edward Montague

I hold it, that a little rebellion, now and then, is a good thing.

Thomas Jefferson

In war, truth is the first casualty.

U. Thant

As long as war is regarded as wicked, it will always have its fascination. When it is looked upon as vulgar, it will cease to be popular.

Oscar Wilde

When one faces a coup d'etat, the first priority is to chop off the hand that holds the weapon. The head comes later.

William Breton

War is carrying out diplomacy in a different way.

Clausewitz

War is the ultimate criminal act.

A tragedy is not a conflict between right and wrong but a conflict between right and right.

Marjorie Phillips

The object of war is not to die for your country but to make the other bastard die for his.

General George S. Patton

Only the dead have seen the end of war.

Plato

WEAKNESS

You cannot run away from a weakness; you must some time fight it or perish; and if that be so, why not now, and where you stand?

Robert Louis Stevenson

Many are saved from sin by being so inept at it.

M. McLaughlin

No sadder proof can be given by a man of his own littleness than disbelief in great men.

Thomas Carlyle

All is vanity – all right, yet who can do without it?

A great empire, like a great cake, is most easily diminished at the edges.

Benjamin Franklin

There is no rock so hard but that a little wave may beat admission in a thousand years.

Tennyson

Only mediocrity is always at its best.

WELL-BEING

Prosperity will be here again when men's trousers begin to bag at the pocket and not at the knees.

I think of myself as a passenger on the *Titanic*. I may not get there, but I'm going first class.

Art Buchwald

Health is a great blessing, contentment the best possession, a true friend the nearest of kin.

WINNING

A good game is one you win.

If winning wasn't important, they wouldn't have score-boards.

If you can't beat them, join them – and then beat them.

The race is not always to the swiftest nor the battle to the strongest . . . but that's the way to back them.

Winning isn't everything; it's the only thing.

Vince Lombardi

He was an awful loser, but a hideous winner.

It is not true that nice guys finish last. Nice guys are winners before the game ever starts.

Addison Walker

You're not paid to do your best; you're paid to win.

Winning is better than losing.

Winning a tennis match is simple: just win the last point.

Pam Shriver

A victory is when you don't have to fight the battle again.

WISDOM

Luxuries are what sensible folk do without until they can afford them.

Adversity makes a man wise – not rich.

We are too soon old and too late smart.

The stupidities of the rich pass for wisdom in the world.

A wise man will live as much within his wit as his income.

Not by age but by capacity is wisdom acquired.

Plautus

The art of being a good chairman at a meeting lies in knowing when to bring it to an end.

Young men think old men are fools; but old men know young men are fools.

Even the fool is wise after the event.

Those who agree with us may not be right, but we admire their astuteness.

A wise man knows everything; a clever man knows everyone.

The wise man looks at all sides of a question; the petty man can only see one side.

Confucius

The wisdom of today may be tomorrow's folly.

Marjorie Phillips

Give instruction to a wise man and he will be yet wiser.

WIVES

If all brides are beautiful, where do plain wives come from?

There is one thing more exasperating than a wife who can cook and won't, and that's the wife who can't cook and will.

Robert Frost

Behind every successful man is an astonished wife.

Never question your wife's judgement. Look at who she married.

R. Greer

Retirement means more husband and less housekeeping.

WOMEN

The silliest woman can manage a clever man; but it needs a very clever woman to manage a fool.

Rudyard Kipling

A youthful figure is what you get when you ask a woman her age.

A career woman is a woman who goes out and earns a man's salary instead of staying at home and taking it away from him.

Sometimes the wolf is at the door at your daughter's invitation.

What every girl should know is a rich young man.

There is nothing sooner dry than women's tears.

When a woman looks young, she wants to look old.
When a woman looks old, she wants to look young.
When a woman looks back, follow her!

No self-made man ever did such a good job that some woman didn't want to make some alterations.

Kim Hubbard

You are not permitted to kill a woman who has wronged you, but nothing forbids you to reflect that she is growing older every minute.

Ambrose Bierce

Women sometimes forgive the man who forces the opportunity, but never a man who misses one.

Charles de Talleyrand-Périgord

Women like a strong, silent man because they think he is listening.

No woman really makes a fool out of a man. She merely gives him the opportunity to develop his natural capacities.

WORK

The number of people who are actually working with their hands on the factory floor goes down every year; the number of people who are working in offices, transport, whatever it is, goes up every year.

If you have no brains, you just have to work.

Some people are still willing to do an honest day's work, but they want a week's pay for it.

A. Preston

The world is full of willing people; some willing to work, the rest willing to let them.

R. Frost

There's a story on the children's page of a trade union journal which begins – 'Once upon a time and a half . . .'

A man is never too tired to tell you how hard he has worked.

Work consists of whatever a body is required to do; play consists of whatever a body is not obliged to do.

Mark Twain

Work expands to fill the time available for its completion.

C. Northcote Parkinson

Work is the crab grass in the lawn of life.

Charles Schulz

Man is so made that he can only find relaxation from one kind of labour by taking up another.

A man is never too busy to talk about how busy he is.

Don't tell me how hard you work. Tell me what you get done.
James Ling

There are two kinds of people; those who do the work and those who take the credit. Try to be in the first group; there is less competition there.
Indira Gandhi

It is not work that kills men; it is worry. Work is healthy.
Henry Ward Beecher

The artist is nothing without the gift, but the gift is nothing without work.
Emile Zola

WORRY

Worry is the interest you pay on a debt not yet due.

You'll die if you worry; you'll die if you don't. Why worry?

Worry affects the circulation, the heart, the glands, the whole nervous system, and profoundly affects the health. I have never known a man who died from overwork, but many who died from doubt.
C. Mayo

Worry never robs tomorrow of its sorrow. It only saps today of its strength.
A.J. Cronin

Worry is like a rocking chair, keeps you going but gets you nowhere.

Not to worry; and if to worry, not to worry unduly.

Abel Walport

Today is the tomorrow you worried about yesterday, and all is well.

Don't panic if you haven't made a table reservation or holiday booking. There is always someone who will take your money.

Samuel J. Henry

As I hurtled through space, one thought kept crossing my mind – every part of this capsule was supplied by the lowest bidder.

John Glenn

If a man can remember what he worried about last week, he has a very good memory.

WORTH

There is hardly anything in the world that some man cannot make a little worse and sell a little cheaper – and the people who consider price only are this man's lawful prey.

John Ruskin

'Nearly' doesn't score points or goals. It just isn't good enough.

All good things are cheap; all bad things are very dear.

Hitting the crossbar doesn't count as a goal, or anything else.

An hour in the morning is worth two in the afternoon.

251

The value of space flight is in the doing of it. The knowledge we will have to gain, the techniques we will have to master, the machines we will have to build – all will bring more material benefit to the Earth's population than any gold or uranium we may find on Mars or Venus.

M.W. Rosen

I often think no man is worth his salt until he has lost and won battles for a principle.

J. Marsh

People can have ability and may have potential, but they do not have worth. Worth is associated with tasks, and worth only starts to have meaning when an element of ability can be matched with an element of requirement.

MAS

Usefulness is the rent we pay for our room on this earth – and many of us are heavily in debt.

The applause of the masses is often a slap in the face for good taste.

A diploma can open the door as a key can, but to stay inside you have to show you're worth something.

The value of a principle is the number of things it will explain.

People only think a thing's worth believing if it's hard to believe.

Armiger Barclay

You don't get what you deserve, you get what you negotiate.

Don King

A true measure of your worth includes all the benefits others have gained from your success.

Cullen Hightower

A commodity is only worth what another man will give for it.

Len Deighton

Isn't it amazing how the value of something plummets whenever you want to sell it?

John Ashley

Not everything that can be counted counts, and not everything that counts can be counted.

Albert Einstein

You find out what something is worth after you have paid for it.

WRITING

A good journalist will invent a story, and then lure the truth towards it.

The strongest memory is weaker than the palest ink.

Never trust to memory what you can put down in writing. Never put down in writing what can be used in evidence against you.

P.J. Kelsey

Why shouldn't truth be stranger than fiction? Fiction, after all, has to make sense.

Mark Twain

Say it with roses, say it with mink; but never, ever, say it with ink.

Jimmy Durante

YOUTH

Youth is a quality, not a matter of circumstances.

Frank Lloyd Wright

I don't feel the least hostile to young people or bothered about them. I don't understand them, but when I was young, people didn't understand me. It's a perfectly natural process.

E.M. Forster

Youth is not an age; it is a state of mind.

Old the proverb, old but true:
Age should think, and Youth should do.

Youth – not a time of life but a state of mind . . . a predominance of courage over timidity, of the appetite for adventure over the love of ease.

Robert F. Kennedy

One good thing about being young is that you are not experienced enough to know that you cannot possibly do the things you are doing.

Gene Brown

Youth – the infinite wisdom of inexperience.

When we talk about missing the way things were when we were young, when we went to the little bakers up the lane and bought hot fresh bread, it is not the ways of living that we are missing. What we are really missing is our youth – and that is gone forever.

Billy Connolly

It is always a mistake to try to impose the rules of an older generation on a new age.

Trevor McDonald